Careers in Focus

BUSINESS

THIRD EDITION

Ferguson
An imprint of Infobase Publishing

Careers in Focus: Business, Third Edition

Ferguson
An imprint of Infobase Publishing
132 West 31st Street
New York NY 10001

Library of Congress Cataloging-in-Publication Data

Careers in focus. Business.—3rd ed.
     p. cm.
   Includes bibliographical references and index.
   ISBN-13: 978-0-8160-8016-8 (hardcover : alk. paper)
   ISBN-10: 0-8160-8016-X (hardcover : alk. paper) 1. Business—Vocational guidance—Juvenile literature.
   HF5381.2.C375 2010
   331.702—dc22
                          2009043359

Ferguson books are available at special discounts when purchased in bulk quantities for businesses, associations, institutions, or sales promotions. Please call our Special Sales Department in New York at (212) 967-8800 or (800) 322-8755.

You can find Ferguson on the World Wide Web at http://www.fergpubco.com

Text design by David Strelecky
Composition by Mary Susan Ryan-Flynn
Cover printed by Art Print, Taylor, PA
Book printed and bound by Maple Press, York, PA
Date printed: May 2010
Printed in the United States of America

10 9 8 7 6 5 4 3 2 1

This book is printed on acid-free paper.

All links and Web addresses were checked and verified to be correct at the time of publication. Because of the dynamic nature of the Web, some addresses and links may have changed since publication and may no longer be valid.

Table of Contents

Introduction

All businesses can be defined as organizations that provide customers with the goods and services they want. There are three main types of businesses in the U.S. economy: manufacturers, merchandisers, and service providers. From skateboards to limousines, virtually everything around you comes from a manufacturing firm of some sort. Merchandisers are businesses that help move products through a channel of distribution to the consumer or end-user. Service providers are businesses that do not sell an actual product but perform a service for a fee. Common examples of service providers are restaurants, dry cleaners, hotels, and hair stylists.

Although there are a wide variety of corporate structures, almost every successful company's structure requires a core group of employees in the areas of production, marketing, finance, human resources, support services, and information technology. Production includes conceptualizing, designing, and creating products and services. Marketing is the process of distributing and promoting the company's product to the right people at the right time. Finance involves the management of a company's money. Human resources or personnel management deals with all aspects of a company's employee culture, including recruiting, hiring, training, evaluating, disciplining, administering benefits, and resolving conflicts. Support services maintain a company's internal workings, including record-keeping, secretarial, and management services. Information technology involves the management of a company's computer systems and technology—including company intranets, networks, firewalls and other security systems, and e-commerce Web sites.

Because it is such a broad category, it is difficult to project growth for business as a whole. While some industries thrive, others decline. There are certain trends, however, that affect business as a whole. For example, all businesses are affected by changes in the economy. When the economy is thriving, consumers have more money to spend, which means they buy more products and services. When the economy suffers a downturn, many businesses suffer as consumers cut back on spending. During tough economic times, many companies downsize and lay off employees in order to stay afloat.

Advances in and increased use of technology also affects all businesses. As industries become more automated, workers with technological know-how are becoming increasingly valuable. A downside of this trend is that as computers cut down on costs and the need for human work, some jobs may be eliminated or combined to reduce costs.

One other major trend is the increasing globalization of the U.S. economy, which will create strong demand for workers with excellent interpersonal skills, a willingness to travel to foreign locales, and fluency in at least one foreign language.

The articles in *Careers in Focus: Business* appear in Ferguson's *Encyclopedia of Careers and Vocational Guidance,* but have been updated and revised with the latest information from the U.S. Department of Labor, professional organizations, and other sources.

The following paragraphs detail the sections and features that appear in the book.

The **Quick Facts** section provides a brief summary of the career including recommended school subjects, personal skills, work environment, minimum educational requirements, salary ranges, certification or licensing requirements, and employment outlook. This section also provides acronyms and identification numbers for the following government classification indexes: the Dictionary of Occupational Titles (DOT), the Guide for Occupational Exploration (GOE), the National Occupational Classification (NOC) Index, and the Occupational Information Network-Standard Occupational Classification System (O*NET-SOC) index. The DOT, GOE, and O*NET-SOC indexes have been created by the U.S. government; the NOC index is Canada's career classification system. Readers can use the identification numbers listed in the Quick Facts section to access further information about a career. Print editions of the DOT (*Dictionary of Occupational Titles.* Indianapolis, Ind.: JIST Works, 1991) and GOE (*Guide for Occupational Exploration.* Indianapolis, Ind.: JIST Works, 2001) are available at libraries. Electronic versions of the NOC (http://www23.hrdc-drhc.gc.ca) and O*NET-SOC (http://online.onetcenter.org) are available on the Internet. When no DOT, GOE, NOC, or O*NET-SOC numbers are present, this means that the U.S. Department of Labor or Human Resources Development Canada have not created a numerical designation for this career. In this instance, you will see the acronym "N/A," or not available.

The **Overview** section is a brief introductory description of the duties and responsibilities involved in this career. Oftentimes, a career may have a variety of job titles. When this is the case, alternative career titles are presented. Employment statistics are also provided, when available. The **History** section describes the history of the particular job as it relates to the overall development of its industry or field. **The Job** describes the primary and secondary duties of the job. **Requirements** discusses high school and postsecondary education and training requirements, any certification or licensing that is necessary, and other personal requirements for success in the job. **Exploring** offers suggestions on how to gain experience in or knowledge of the particular job before making a firm educational and financial commitment. The focus is on what can be done while still in high school (or in the early years of college) to gain a better understanding of the job. The **Employers** section gives an overview of typical places of employment for the job. **Starting Out** discusses the best ways to land that first job, be it through the college career services office, newspaper ads, Internet employment sites, or personal contact. The **Advancement** section describes what kind of career path to expect from the job and how to get there. **Earnings** lists salary ranges and describes the typical fringe benefits. The **Work Environment** section describes the typical surroundings and conditions of employment—whether indoors or outdoors, noisy or quiet, social or independent. Also discussed are typical hours worked, any seasonal fluctuations, and the stresses and strains of the job. The **Outlook** section summarizes the job in terms of the general economy and industry projections. For the most part, Outlook information is obtained from the U.S. Bureau of Labor Statistics and is supplemented by information gathered from professional associations. Job growth terms follow those used in the *Occupational Outlook Handbook*. Growth described as "much faster than the average" means an increase of 21 percent or more. Growth described as "faster than the average" means an increase of 14 to 20 percent. Growth described as "about as fast as the average" means an increase of 7 to 13 percent. Growth described as "more slowly than the average" means an increase of 3 to 6 percent. "Little or no change" means a decrease of 2 percent to an increase of 2 percent. "Decline" means a decrease of 3 percent or more. Each article ends with **For More Information,** which lists organizations that provide information on training, education, internships, scholarships, and job placement.

Careers in Focus: Business also includes photos, informative sidebars, and interviews with professionals in the field.

As you explore the wide variety of careers in business that are presented in this book, consider which of them might best suit your personality, strengths, and general career goals. Be sure to contact the organizations listed at the end of each article for more information.

Accountants and Auditors

OVERVIEW

Accountants compile, analyze, verify, and prepare financial records, including profit and loss statements, balance sheets, cost studies, and tax reports. Accountants may specialize in areas such as auditing, tax work, cost accounting, budgeting and control, or systems and procedures. Accountants may also specialize in a particular business or field; for example, *agricultural accountants* specialize in drawing up and analyzing financial statements for farmers and for farm equipment companies. *Auditors* examine and verify financial records to ensure that they are accurate, complete, and in compliance with federal laws. There are approximately 1.3 million accountants and auditors employed in the United States.

HISTORY

Accounting records and bookkeeping methods have been used from early history to the present. Accounting records were kept in ancient Babylonia (modern-day Iraq) as far back as 3600 B.C.; evidence of accounting practices have also been found in ancient Egyptian, Greek, and Roman civilizations.

Modern accounting began with the technique of double-entry bookkeeping, which was developed in the 15th and 16th centuries by Luca Pacioli, an Italian mathematician. After the industrial revolution, business grew more complex. As government and industrial institutions developed in the 19th and 20th centuries, accurate records and information were needed to assist in making decisions on economic and management policies.

The accounting profession in the United States dates back only to 1880, when English and Scottish investors began buying stock in American companies. To keep an eye on their investments, these investors sent over accountants, who realized the great potential that existed in the accounting field and stayed on to establish their own businesses. Federal legislation, such as the income tax established in 1913, helped cause the ongoing growth in the accounting field that has made the profession instrumental to all business.

Accountants have long been considered "bean counters," and their work has been written off by outsiders as routine and boring. However, their image, once associated with death, taxes, and bad news, is making a turnaround. Accountants now do much more than prepare financial statements and record business transactions. Technology now counts the "beans," allowing accountants to analyze and interpret the results. Their work has expanded to encompass challenging and creative tasks such as computing costs and efficiency gains of new technologies, participating in strategies for mergers and acquisitions, supervising quality management, and designing and using information systems to track financial performance.

THE JOB

Accountants' duties depend on the size and nature of the company in which they are employed. The major fields of employment are public, private, and government accounting.

Public accountants work independently on a fee basis or as members of an accounting firm, and they perform a variety of tasks for businesses or individuals. These may include auditing accounts and records, preparing and certifying financial statements, conducting financial investigations and furnishing testimony in legal matters, and assisting in formulating budget policies and procedures.

Private accountants, sometimes called *industrial* or *management accountants,* handle financial records of the firms at which they are employed.

Government accountants work on the financial records of government agencies or, when necessary, they audit the records of private companies. In the federal government, many accountants are employed as *bank examiners, Internal Revenue Service agents and investigators,* as well as in regular accounting positions.

Within these fields, accountants can specialize in a variety of areas.

General accountants supervise, install, and devise general accounting, budget, and cost systems. They maintain records, balance books, and prepare and analyze statements on all financial aspects of business. Administrative officers use this information to make sound business decisions.

Budget accountants review expenditures of departments within a firm to make sure expenses allotted are not exceeded. They also aid in drafting budgets and may devise and install budget control systems.

Cost accountants determine unit costs of products or services by analyzing records and depreciation data. They classify and record all operating costs so that management can control expenditures.

Property accountants keep records of equipment, buildings, and other property owned or leased by a company. They prepare mortgage schedules and payment plans as well as appreciation or depreciation statements, which are used for income tax purposes.

Environmental accountants help utilities, manufacturers, and chemical companies set up preventive systems to ensure environmental compliance and provide assistance in the event that legal issues arise.

Systems accountants design and set up special accounting systems for organizations whose needs cannot be handled by standardized procedures. This may involve installing automated or computerized accounting processes and includes instructing personnel in the new methods.

Forensic accountants and auditors use accounting principles and theories to support or oppose claims being made in litigation.

Tax accountants prepare federal, state, and local tax returns of an individual, business, or corporation according to prescribed rates, laws, and regulations. They may also conduct research on the effects of taxes on firm operations and recommend changes to reduce taxes. This is one of the most intricate fields of accounting, and many accountants therefore specialize in one particular phase such as corporate, individual income, or property tax.

Assurance accountants help improve the quality of information for clients in assurance services areas such as electronic commerce, risk assessment, and elder care. This information may be financial or nonfinancial in nature.

Auditors ensure that financial records are accurate, complete, and in compliance with federal laws. To do so they review items in original entry books, including purchase orders, tax returns, billing statements, and other important documents. Auditors may also prepare financial statements for clients and suggest ways to improve productivity and profits. *Internal auditors* conduct the same kind of examination and evaluation for one particular company. Because they are salaried employees of that company, their financial audits must then be certified by a qualified independent auditor. Internal auditors also review procedures and controls, appraise the efficiency and effectiveness of operations, and make sure their companies comply with corporate policies and government regulations.

Tax auditors review financial records and other information provided by taxpayers to determine the appropriate tax liability. State and federal tax auditors usually work in government offices, but they may perform a field audit in a taxpayer's home or office.

Revenue agents are employed by the federal government to examine selected income tax returns and, when necessary, conduct field audits and investigations to verify the information reported and adjust the tax liability accordingly.

Chief bank examiners enforce good banking practices throughout a state. They schedule bank examinations to ensure that financial institutions comply with state laws and, in certain cases, they take steps to protect a bank's solvency and the interests of its depositors and shareholders.

REQUIREMENTS

High School

If you are interested in an accounting career, you must be very proficient in arithmetic and basic algebra. Familiarity with computers and their applications is equally important. Course work in English and communications will also be beneficial.

Postsecondary Training

Postsecondary training in accounting may be obtained in a wide variety of institutions such as private business schools, junior colleges, universities, and correspondence schools. A bachelor's degree with a major in accounting, or a related field such as economics, is highly recommended by professional associations for those entering the field and is required by all states before taking the licensing exam. It is possible, however, to become a successful accountant by completing a program at any of the above-mentioned institutions. A four-year college curriculum usually includes about two years of liberal arts courses, a year of general business subjects, and a year of specific accounting work. Better positions, particularly in public accounting, require a bachelor's degree with a major in accounting. Large public accounting firms often prefer people with a master's degree in accounting. For beginning positions in accounting, the federal government requires four years of college (including 24 semester hours in accounting or auditing) or an equivalent combination of education and experience.

Certification or Licensing

A large percentage of accountants and auditors are certified. *Certified public accountants* (CPAs) must pass a qualifying examination and hold a certificate issued by the state in which they wish to practice. In most states, a college degree is required for admission to the CPA examinations; a few states allow candidates to substitute years of public accounting experience for the college degree requirement. Currently 42 states and the District of Columbia require CPA candidates to have 150 hours of education, which is an additional 30 hours beyond the standard bachelor's degree. Four additional states plan to enact the 150-hour requirement in the future. These criteria can be met by combining an undergraduate accounting program with graduate study or by participating in an integrated five-year professional accounting program. You can obtain information from a state board of accountancy or check out the Web site of the American Institute of Certified Public Accountants (AICPA) to read about new regulations and review last year's exam.

The Uniform CPA Examination administered by the AICPA is used by all states. Nearly all states require at least two years of public accounting experience or its equivalent before a CPA certificate can be earned.

The AICPA offers additional credentialing programs (involving a test and additional requirements) for members with valid CPA certificates. These designations include accredited in business valuation, certified information technology professional, and personal financial specialist. These credentials indicate that a CPA has developed skills in nontraditional areas in which accountants are starting to play larger roles.

Some accountants seek out other credentials. Those who have earned a bachelor's degree, passed a four-part examination, agreed to meet continuing education requirements, and have at least two years of experience in management accounting may become a certified management accountant through the Institute of Management Accounting.

The Accreditation Council for Accountancy and Taxation confers the following designations: accredited business accountant or accredited business adviser, accredited tax preparer, accredited tax adviser, and elder care specialist.

To become a certified internal auditor, college graduates with two years of experience in internal auditing must pass a four-part

Accounting Education/ Employment: An Overview

- Enrollments in college accounting programs increased by 19 percent from 2003–2004 to 2006–2007.
- A significant amount of enrollment growth occurred at the bachelor's degree level.
- Minority students made up 26 percent of bachelor's degree enrollments and 20 percent of master's degree enrollments from 2003–2004 to 2006–2007.
- Public accounting firms hire 34 percent of new graduates with bachelor's degrees in accounting and 70 percent of graduates with master's degree in accounting.
- Sixty-seven percent of the largest public accounting firms predict that they will need to hire more accounting graduates in coming years.

Source: 2008 Trends in the Supply of Accounting Graduates and the Demand for Public Accounting Recruits, American Institute of Certified Public Accountants

examination given by the Institute of Internal Auditors (IIA). The IIA also offers the following specialty certifications: certified financial services auditor and certified government auditing professional. Visit the IIA's Web site for more information.

The designation certified information systems auditor is conferred by the Information Systems Audit and Control Association to candidates who pass an examination and who have five years of experience auditing electronic data processing systems.

Other organizations, such as the Banking Administration Institute, confer specialized auditing designations.

Other Requirements

To be a successful accountant you will need strong mathematical, analytical, and problem-solving skills. You need to be able to think logically and to interpret facts and figures accurately. Effective oral and written communication is also essential in working with both clients and management.

Other important skills are attentiveness to detail, patience, and industriousness. Business acumen and the ability to generate clientele are crucial to service-oriented businesses, as are honesty, dedication, and a respect for the work of others.

EXPLORING

The American Institute of Certified Public Accountants offers an excellent Web site (http://www.startheregoplaces.com), which will help you learn more about the field. It features information on recommended high school courses, important personal skills for accountants, postsecondary training programs, scholarships, internships, and career options in the field.

If you think a career as an accountant or auditor might be for you, try working in a retail business, either part time or during the summer. Working at the cash register or even at pricing products as a stockperson is good introductory experience. You should also consider working as a treasurer for a student organization, which requires learning financial planning and money management skills. It may be possible to gain some experience by volunteering with local groups such as religious organizations and small businesses. You should also stay abreast of news in the field by reading trade magazines and checking out the industry Web sites of the AICPA and other accounting associations. The AICPA has numerous free educational publications available.

EMPLOYERS

Approximately 1.3 million people are employed as accountants and auditors. Accountants and auditors work throughout private industry and government. About 21 percent work for accounting, tax preparation, bookkeeping, and payroll services firms. Approximately 10 percent are self-employed.

STARTING OUT

Junior public accountants usually start in jobs with routine duties such as counting cash, verifying calculations, and other detailed numerical work. In private accounting, beginners are likely to start as cost accountants and junior internal auditors. They may also enter in clerical positions as cost clerks, ledger clerks, and timekeepers or as trainees in technical or junior executive positions. In the federal government, most beginners are hired as trainees at the GS-5 level after passing the civil service exam.

Some state CPA societies arrange internships for accounting majors, and some offer scholarships and loan programs.

You might also visit the Landing a Job section of the AICPA's Web site (http://www.aicpa.org/YoungCPANetwork/Planning_Developing. htm). It has detailed information on accounting careers, hiring trends, job search strategies, résumés and cover letters, and job interviews. The section also has a list of internship opportunities for students. The Jobs & Internships section of the AICPA's career exploration Web site (http://www.startheregoplaces.com/jobs) also offers useful information for those new to the field.

ADVANCEMENT

Talented accountants and auditors can advance quickly. Junior public accountants usually advance to senior positions within several years and to managerial positions soon after. Those successful in dealing with top-level management may eventually become supervisors, managers, and partners in larger firms or go into independent practice. However, only 2 to 3 percent of new hires advance to audit manager, tax manager, or partner.

Private accountants in firms may become audit managers, tax managers, cost accounting managers, or controllers, depending on their specialty. Some become controllers, treasurers, or corporation presidents. Others on the finance side may rise to become managers of financial planning and analysis or treasurers.

Federal government trainees are usually promoted within a year or two. Advancement to controller and to higher administrative positions is ultimately possible.

Although advancement may be rapid for skilled accountants, especially in public accounting, those with inadequate academic or professional training are often assigned to routine jobs and find it difficult to obtain promotions. All accountants find it necessary to continue their study of accounting and related areas in their spare time. Even those who have already obtained college degrees, gained experience, and earned a CPA certificate may spend many hours studying to keep up with new industry developments. Thousands of practicing accountants enroll in formal courses offered by universities and professional associations to specialize in certain areas of accounting, broaden or update their professional skills, and become eligible for advancement and promotion.

EARNINGS

Beginning salaries for accountants with a bachelor's degree averaged $47,421 per year in 2007, according to the National Association of Colleges and Employers. General accountants at large companies with up to one year of experience earned between $36,750 and $44,750 per year, according to a 2008 survey by Robert Half International. Some experienced internal auditors may earn between $58,250 and $84,000 per year, depending on such factors as their education level, the size of the firm, and the firm's location.

According to the U.S. Department of Labor, accountants and auditors had median annual earnings of $57,060 in 2007. The lowest paid 10 percent earned less than $35,570, and the highest paid 10 percent earned more than $98,220. In the federal government, the average starting salary for junior accountants and auditors was $28,862 in 2007. Some entry-level positions paid slightly more if the candidate had an advanced degree or superior academic performance. Accountants working for the federal government in supervisory and management positions had average salaries of $78,665 per year in 2007; auditors averaged $83,322. Although government accountants and auditors make less than those in other areas, they do receive more benefits.

Accountants in large firms and with large corporations receive typical benefits including paid vacation and sick days, insurance, and savings and pension plans. Employees in smaller companies generally receive fewer fringe benefits.

WORK ENVIRONMENT

Accounting is a desk job, and a 40-hour (or longer) workweek can be expected in public and private accounting. Although computer work is replacing paperwork, the job can be routine and monotonous, and concentration and attention to detail are critical. Public accountants experience considerable pressure during the tax period, which runs from November to April, and they may have to work long hours during tax season. There is potential for stress aside from tax season, as accountants can be responsible for managing multimillion-dollar finances with no margin for error. Self-employed accountants and those working for a small firm can expect to work longer hours; 40 percent work more than 50 hours per week, compared to 20 percent of public and private accountants.

In smaller firms, most of the public accountant's work is performed in the client's office. A considerable amount of travel is often necessary to service a wide variety of businesses. In a larger firm, however, an accountant may have very little client contact, spending more time interacting with the accounting team.

OUTLOOK

Employment of accountants and auditors is expected to grow faster than the average for all occupations through 2016, according to the

U.S. Department of Labor. This is due to business growth, changing tax and finance laws, and increased scrutiny of financial practices across all businesses. There have been several notable scandals in the accounting industry in recent years, and this accounts for much of the increased scrutiny and changing legislation in this industry.

As firms specialize their services, accountants will need to follow suit. Firms will seek out accountants with experience in marketing and proficiency in computer systems to build management consulting practices. As trade increases, so will the demand for CPAs with international specialties and foreign language skills. CPAs with an engineering degree would be well equipped to specialize in environmental accounting. Other accounting specialties that will enjoy good prospects include assurance and forensic accounting.

The number of CPAs dropped off a bit after most states embraced the 150-hour standard for CPA education. However, numbers are once again starting to rise as students realize the many opportunities this industry holds, especially in the wake of recent accounting scandals. CPAs with valid licenses should experience favorable job prospects for the foreseeable future. Pursuing advanced degrees and certifications will also greatly increase one's chances of finding employment.

Accounting jobs are more secure than most during economic downswings. Despite fluctuations in the nation's economy, there will always be a need to manage financial information, especially as the number, size, and complexity of business transactions increases. However, competition for jobs will remain, certification requirements will become more rigorous, and accountants and auditors with the highest degrees will be the most competitive.

FOR MORE INFORMATION

For information on accreditation and testing, contact
Accreditation Council for Accountancy and Taxation
1010 North Fairfax Street
Alexandria, VA 22314-1574
Tel: 888-289-7763
Email: info@acatcredentials.org
http://www.acatcredentials.org

For information on the Uniform CPA Examination and student membership, contact
American Institute of Certified Public Accountants
1211 Avenue of the Americas

New York, NY 10036-8775
Tel: 212-596-6200
http://www.aicpa.org

For information on accredited programs in accounting, contact
Association to Advance Collegiate Schools of Business
777 South Harbour Island Boulevard, Suite 750
Tampa, FL 33602-5730
Tel: 813-769-6500
http://www.aacsb.edu

For information on certification for bank auditors, contact
Banking Administration Institute
115 South LaSalle Street, Suite 3300
Chicago, IL 60603-3801
Email: info@bai.org
http://www.bai.org

For more information on women in accounting, contact
Educational Foundation for Women in Accounting
136 South Keowee Street
Dayton, OH 45402-2241
Tel: 937-424-3391
Email: info@efwa.org
http://www.efwa.org

For information on certification, contact
Information Systems Audit and Control Association
3701 Algonquin Road, Suite 1010
Rolling Meadows, IL 60008-3124
Tel: 847-253-1545
Email: certification@isaca.org
http://www.isaca.org

For information on internal auditing and certification, contact
Institute of Internal Auditors
247 Maitland Avenue
Altamonte Springs, FL 32701-4201
Tel: 407-937-1100
Email: iia@theiia.org
http://www.theiia.org

For information about management accounting and the CMA designation, as well as student membership, contact

Institute of Management Accountants
10 Paragon Drive
Montvale, NJ 07645-1718
Tel: 800-638-4427
Email: ima@imanet.org
http://www.imanet.org

Billing Clerks

OVERVIEW

Billing clerks produce and process bills and collect payments from customers. They enter transactions in business ledgers or spreadsheets, write and send invoices, and verify purchase orders. They post items in accounts payable or receivable, calculate customer charges, and verify the company's rates for certain products and services. Billing clerks must make sure that all entries are accurate and up-to-date. At the end of the fiscal year, they may work with auditors to clarify billing procedures and answer questions about specific accounts. There are approximately 542,000 billing clerks employed in the United States.

HISTORY

The need to record business transactions has existed ever since people began to engage in business and commerce. As far back as 3600 B.C., Sumerians in Mesopotamia recorded sales and bills for customers on clay tablets. Wealthy traders of early Egyptian and Babylonian civilizations often trained their slaves to make markings on clay tablets to keep track of the traders' purchases and sales.

With the rise of monarchies in Europe, billing clerks were needed to record the business transactions of kings, queens, and rich merchants and to monitor the status of the royal treasury. During the Middle Ages, monks carried out the tasks of billing clerks. As the industrial revolution spread across Europe, increasing commercial transactions, billing clerks became a necessary part of the workforce.

QUICK FACTS

School Subjects
Business
English
Mathematics

Personal Skills
Following instructions
Technical/scientific

Work Environment
Primarily indoors
Primarily one location

Minimum Education Level
High school diploma

Salary Range
$20,000 to $29,970 to $43,160+

Certification or Licensing
None available

Outlook
More slowly than the average

DOT
214

GOE
09.03.01

NOC
1431

O*NET-SOC
43-3021.00, 43-3021.02, 43-3021.03

Computer technology has changed the way clerks record transactions today, allowing for billing information and financial transactions to be recorded electronically, eliminating the need for paperwork. But billing clerks continue to occupy a central role in the business world, managing the day-to-day inner workings of company finance.

THE JOB

Billing clerks are responsible for keeping records and up-to-date accounts of all business transactions. They type and send bills for services or products and update files to reflect payments. They also review incoming invoices to ensure that the requested products have been delivered and that the billing statements are accurate and paid on time.

Billing clerks set up shipping and receiving dates. They check customer orders before shipping to make sure they are complete and that all costs, shipping charges, taxes, and credits are included. Billing clerks are also troubleshooters. They contact suppliers or customers when payments are past due or incorrect and help solve the minor problems that invariably occur in the course of business transactions.

Billing clerks enter all transaction information into the firm's account ledger. This ledger lists all the company's transactions, such as items bought or sold, as well as the credit terms and payment and receiving dates. As payments come in, the billing clerk applies credit to customer accounts and applies any applicable discounts. All correspondence is carefully filed for future reference. Nearly all of this work is done using spreadsheets and computer databases.

The specific duties of billing clerks vary according to the nature of the business in which they work. In an insurance company, the transaction sheet will reflect when and how much customers must pay on their insurance bills. Billing clerks in hospitals compile itemized charges, calculate insurance benefits, and process insurance claims. In accounting, law, and consulting firms, they calculate billable hours and work completed.

Billing clerks are also often responsible for preparing summary statements of financial status, profit-and-loss statements, and payroll lists and deductions. These reports are submitted periodically to company management, who can then gauge the company's financial performance. Clerks may also write company checks, compute federal tax reports, and tabulate personnel profit shares.

Billing clerks may have a specific role within a company. These areas of specialization include the following:

Invoice-control clerks post items in accounts payable or receivable ledgers and verify the accuracy of billing data.

Passenger rate clerks compute fare information for business trips and then provide this information to business personnel.

COD (cash-on-delivery) clerks calculate and record the amount of money collected on COD delivery routes.

Interline clerks compute and pay freight charges for airlines or other transportation agencies that carry freight or passengers as part of a business transaction.

Settlement clerks compute and pay shippers for materials forwarded to a company.

Billing-control clerks compute and pay utility companies for services provided.

Rate reviewers compile data relating to utility costs for management officials.

Services clerks compute and pay tariff charges for boats or ships used to transport materials.

Foreign clerks compute duties, tariffs, and price conversions of exported and imported products.

Billing-machine operators mechanically prepare bills and statements.

Deposit-refund clerks prepare bills for utility customers.

Raters calculate premiums to be paid by customers of insurance companies.

Telegraph-service raters compute costs for sending telegrams.

Billing clerks may work in one specific area or they may be responsible for several areas.

REQUIREMENTS

High School

A high school diploma is usually sufficient for an entry-level billing clerk position, although taking a few business courses in computer operations and bookkeeping will make you a more desirable candidate to employers. In high school, take English, communications, and business writing courses. Computer science and mathematics courses will also prepare you for this career. Some companies test their applicants on math, typing, and computer skills, and others offer on-the-job training.

Postsecondary Training

Community colleges, junior colleges, and vocational schools often offer business education courses that can provide you with additional training.

Employment/Earnings for Billing Clerks by Industry, 2007

Employer	# Employed	Annual Mean Earnings
Offices of physicians	91,310	$31,110
General medical and surgical hospitals	42,130	$30,620
Accounting, tax preparation, bookkeeping, and payroll services	34,850	$30,970
Management of companies and enterprises	22,530	$32,240
Offices of other health practitioners	16,170	$29,540
Legal services	7,480	$36,950

Source: U.S. Department of Labor

Other Requirements

If you hope to be a billing clerk, you should have excellent mathematical and organizational skills, be detail oriented, and be able to concentrate on repetitive tasks for long periods of time. In addition, you should be dependable, honest, and trustworthy in dealing with confidential financial matters.

EXPLORING

You can gain experience in this field by taking on clerical or bookkeeping responsibilities with a school club, student government, or other extracurricular activities. If you are interested in the field, you can work in retail operations, either part time or during the summer. Working at the cash register or even pricing products as a stockperson is a good introductory experience. It may also be possible to gain some experience by volunteering to help maintain the bookkeeping records for local groups, such as religious organizations and small businesses.

EMPLOYERS

Employers of billing clerks include hospitals, insurance companies, banks, manufacturers, and utility companies. Of the approximately

542,000 billing clerks employed in the United States, more than one-third are employed in the health care field. Wholesale and resale trade industries also employ a large number of billing clerks. Businesses that provide billing services for other companies employ about 11 percent of these workers—mainly in the accounting, administrative and support services, bookkeeping, payroll services, and tax preparation industries. Approximately 16 percent of billing clerks work part time.

STARTING OUT

Your high school job placement or guidance office can help you find employment opportunities or establish job contacts after you graduate. You may also find specific jobs through classified newspaper advertisements. Most companies provide on-the-job training for entry-level billing clerks to explain to them company procedures and policies and to teach them the basic tasks of the job. During the first month, billing clerks work with experienced personnel.

ADVANCEMENT

Billing clerks usually begin by handling routine tasks such as recording transactions. With experience, they may advance to more complex assignments—which entail computer training in databases and spreadsheets—and assume a greater responsibility for the work as a whole. With additional training and education, billing clerks can be promoted to positions as bookkeepers, accountants, or auditors. Billing clerks with strong leadership and management skills can advance to group manager or supervisor. There is a high turnover rate in this field, which increases the chance of promotion for employees with ability and initiative.

EARNINGS

Salaries for billing clerks depend on the size and geographic location of the company as well as the employee's skills. Starting salaries for an employee with little experience may be around $20,000 per year. Full-time billing and posting clerks earned a median hourly wage of $14.41 in 2007, according to the U.S. Department of Labor. For full-time work at 40 hours per week, this hourly wage translates into an annual income of approximately $29,970. Some bill and account collectors may earn a commission based on the number of cases they close in a given time period. Billing clerks with high levels of expertise and management responsibilities may make $43,160 per year or more. Full-time workers also receive paid vacation, health insurance, and other benefits.

WORK ENVIRONMENT

Like most office workers, billing clerks usually work in modern office environments and average 40 hours of work per week. Billing clerks spend most of their time behind a desk, and their work can be routine and repetitive. Working long hours in front of a computer can often cause eyestrain, backaches, and headaches, although efforts are being made to reduce physical problems with ergonomically correct equipment. Billing clerks should enjoy systematic and orderly work and have a keen eye for numerical detail. While much of the work is solitary, billing clerks often interact with accountants and management and may work under close supervision.

OUTLOOK

The U.S. Department of Labor predicts that employment for billing clerks will grow more slowly than the average for all careers through 2016. A number of factors will contribute to this slow growth rate. For example, technological advancements—computers, electronic billing, and automated payment methods—will streamline operations and result in the need for fewer workers. The rising popularity of billing via the Internet will also eliminate the number of billing clerks needed in many businesses. Additionally, the responsibilities of billing clerks may be combined with those of other positions. In smaller companies, for example, accounting clerks will make use of billing software, making billing clerks obsolete. Many job openings will result from the need to replace workers who have left for different jobs or other reasons. The health care sector should remain a large employer in this field.

FOR MORE INFORMATION

For information on union membership, contact
Office and Professional Employees International Union
265 West 14th Street, 6th Floor
New York, NY 10011-7103
Tel: 800-346-7348
http://www.opeiu.org

For free office career and salary information, visit the following Web site:
OfficeTeam
http://www.officeteam.com

Bookkeeping and Accounting Clerks

OVERVIEW

Bookkeeping and accounting clerks record financial transactions for government, business, and other organizations. They compute, classify, record, and verify numerical data in order to develop and maintain accurate financial records. There are approximately 2.1 million bookkeeping, accounting, and auditing clerks employed in the United States.

HISTORY

The history of bookkeeping developed along with the growth of business and industrial enterprise. The first known records of bookkeeping date back to 3600 B.C., when the Babylonians used pointed sticks to mark accounts on clay slabs. By 3000 B.C., Middle Eastern and Egyptian cultures employed a system of numbers to record merchants' transactions of the grain and farm products that were distributed from storage warehouses. The growth of intricate trade systems brought about the necessity for bookkeeping systems.

Sometime after the start of the 13th century, the decimal numeration system was introduced in Europe, simplifying bookkeeping record systems. The merchants of Venice—one of the busiest trading centers in the world at that time—are credited with the invention of the double entry bookkeeping method that is widely used today.

As industry in the United States expands and grows more complex, simpler and quicker bookkeeping methods and procedures have evolved. Technological developments include bookkeeping machines, computer hardware and software, and electronic data processing.

THE JOB

Bookkeeping workers keep systematic records and current accounts of financial transactions for businesses, institutions, industries, charities, and other organizations. The bookkeeping records of a firm or business are a vital part of its operational procedures because these records reflect the business' assets and liabilities, as well as its profits and losses.

Bookkeepers record these business transactions daily in spreadsheets on computer databases, and accounting clerks often input the information. The practice of posting accounting records directly onto ledger sheets, in journals, or on other types of written accounting forms is decreasing as computerized record keeping becomes more widespread. In small businesses, bookkeepers sort and record all the sales slips, bills, check stubs, inventory lists, and requisition lists. They compile figures for cash receipts, accounts payable and receivable, and profits and losses.

Accounting clerks handle the clerical accounting work; they enter and verify transaction data and compute and record various charges. They may also monitor loans and accounts payable and receivable. More advanced clerks may reconcile billing vouchers, while senior workers review invoices and statements.

Accountants set up bookkeeping systems and use bookkeepers' balance sheets to prepare periodic summary statements of financial transactions. Management relies heavily on these bookkeeping records to interpret the organization's overall performance and uses them to make important business decisions. The records are also necessary to file income tax reports and prepare quarterly reports for stockholders.

Bookkeeping and accounting clerks work in retail and wholesale businesses, manufacturing firms, hospitals, schools, charities, and other types of institutional agencies. Many clerks are classified as financial institution bookkeeping and accounting clerks, insurance firm bookkeeping and accounting clerks, hotel bookkeeping and accounting clerks, and railroad bookkeeping and accounting clerks.

General bookkeepers and *general-ledger bookkeepers* are usually employed in smaller business operations. They may perform all the analysis, maintain the financial records, and complete any other tasks that are involved in keeping a full set of bookkeeping records. These employees may have other general office duties, such as mailing statements, answering telephone calls, and filing materials. *Audit clerks* verify figures and may be responsible for sending them on to an audit clerk supervisor.

In large companies, an accountant may supervise a department of bookkeepers who perform more specialized work. *Billing and rate clerks* and *fixed capital clerks* may post items in accounts payable or receivable ledgers, make out bills and invoices, or verify the company's rates for certain products and services. *Account information clerks* prepare reports, compile payroll lists and deductions, write company checks, and compute federal tax reports or personnel profit shares. Large companies may employ workers to organize, record, and compute many other types of financial information.

In large business organizations, bookkeepers and accountants may be classified by grades, such as Bookkeeper I or II. The job classification determines their responsibilities.

REQUIREMENTS

High School
In order to be a bookkeeper, you will need at least a high school diploma. It will be helpful to have a background in business mathematics, business writing, typing, and computer training. Pay particular attention to developing sound English and communication skills along with mathematical abilities.

Postsecondary Training
Some employers prefer people who have completed a junior college curriculum or those who have attended a post–high school business training program. In many instances, employers offer on-the-job training for various types of entry-level positions. In some areas, work-study programs are available in which schools, in cooperation with businesses, offer part-time, practical on-the-job training combined with academic study. These programs often help students find immediate employment in similar work after graduation. Local business schools may also offer evening courses.

Certification or Licensing
The American Institute of Professional Bookkeepers offers voluntary certification to bookkeepers who have at least two years of full-time experience (or the part-time or freelance equivalent), pass an examination, and sign a code of ethics. Bookkeepers who fulfill these requirements may use the designation certified bookkeeper.

Other Requirements

Bookkeepers need strong mathematical skills and organizational abilities, and they have to be able to concentrate on detailed work. The work is quite sedentary and often tedious, and you should not mind long hours sitting behind a desk. You should be methodical, accurate, and orderly and enjoy working on detailed tasks. Employers look for honest, discreet, and trustworthy individuals when placing their business in someone else's hands.

Once you are employed as a bookkeeping and accounting clerk, some places of business may require you to have union membership. Larger unions include the Office and Professional Employees International Union; the International Union of Electronic, Electrical, Salaried, Machine, and Furniture Workers-Communications Workers of America; and the American Federation of State, County, and Municipal Employees. Also, depending on the business, clerks may be represented by the same union as other manufacturing employees.

EXPLORING

You can gain experience in bookkeeping by participating in work-study programs or by obtaining part-time or summer work in entry-level bookkeeping jobs or related office work. Any retail experience dealing with cash management, pricing, or customer service is also valuable.

You can also volunteer to manage the books for extracurricular student groups. Managing income or cash flow for a club or acting as treasurer for student government are excellent ways to gain experience in maintaining financial records. Other options are visiting local small businesses to observe their work and talking to representatives of schools that offer business-training courses.

EMPLOYERS

Of the approximately 2.1 million bookkeeping, auditing, and accounting clerks, many work for personnel supplying companies; that is, those companies that provide part-time or temporary office workers. Approximately 24 percent of bookkeeping and accounting clerks work part time, according to the U.S. Department of Labor. Many others are employed by government agencies and organizations that provide educational, health, business, and social services.

STARTING OUT

You may find jobs or establish contacts with businesses that are interested in interviewing graduates through your guidance or career services offices. A work-study program or internship may result in an offer of a full-time job. Business schools and junior colleges generally provide assistance to their graduates in locating employment.

You may locate job opportunities by applying directly to firms or responding to ads in newspaper classified sections. State employment agencies and private employment bureaus can also assist in the job search process.

ADVANCEMENT

Bookkeeping workers generally begin their employment by performing routine tasks, such as the simple recording of transactions. Beginners may start as entry-level clerks, cashiers, bookkeeping machine operators, office assistants, or typists. With experience, they may advance to more complex assignments that include computer training in databases and spreadsheets and assume a greater responsibility for the work as a whole.

With experience and education, clerks become department heads or office managers. Further advancement to positions such as office or division manager, department head, accountant, or auditor is possible with a college degree and years of experience. There is a high turnover rate in this field, which increases the promotion opportunities for employees with ability and initiative.

EARNINGS

According to the U.S. Department of Labor, bookkeepers and accounting clerks earned a median income of $31,560 per year in 2007. Earnings are also influenced by such factors as the size of the city or town where they work and the size and type of business for which they are employed. Clerks just starting out earn annual salaries of approximately $20,310. Those with one or two years of college generally earn higher starting wages. Top-paying jobs averaged $47,580 or more per year.

Employees usually receive six to eight paid holidays yearly and one week of paid vacation after six to 12 months of service. Paid vacations may increase to four weeks or more, depending on length of service and place of employment. Fringe benefits may include health and life insurance, sick leave, and retirement plans.

WORK ENVIRONMENT

The majority of office workers, including bookkeeping workers, usually work a 40-hour week, although some employees may work a 35- to 37-hour week. Bookkeeping and accounting clerks usually work in typical office settings. They are more likely to have a cubicle than an office. While the work pace is steady, it can also be routine and repetitive, especially in large companies where the employee is often assigned only one or two specialized job duties.

Attention to numerical details can be physically demanding, as the work can produce eyestrain and nervousness. While bookkeepers usually work with other people and sometimes under close supervision, they can expect to spend most of their day behind a desk; this may seem confining to people who need more variety and stimulation in their work. In addition, the constant attention to detail and the need for accuracy can place considerable responsibility on the worker and cause much stress.

OUTLOOK

The growing number of financial transactions and the implementation of the Sarbanes-Oxley Act of 2002, which requires more accurate reporting of financial data for public companies, have created steady employment growth for bookkeeping and accounting clerks. Employment of bookkeeping and accounting clerks is expected to grow about as fast as the average for all occupations through 2016, according to the U.S. Department of Labor.

There will be numerous replacement job openings, since the turnover rate in this occupation is high. Offices are centralizing their operations, setting up one center to manage all accounting needs in a single location. As more companies trim back their workforces, opportunities for temporary work should continue to grow.

The automation of office functions will continue to improve overall worker productivity, which may limit job growth in some settings. Excellent computer skills and professional certification will be vital to securing a job.

FOR MORE INFORMATION

For information on certification and career opportunities, contact
American Institute of Professional Bookkeepers
6001 Montrose Road, Suite 500
Rockville, MD 20852-4873
Tel: 800-622-0121

Email: info@aipb.org
http://www.aipb.org

For information on accredited educational programs, contact
Association to Advance Collegiate Schools of Business
777 South Harbour Island Boulevard, Suite 750
Tampa, FL 33602-5730
Tel: 813-769-6500
http://www.aacsb.edu

For more information on women in accounting, contact
Educational Foundation for Women in Accounting
136 South Keowee Street
Dayton, OH 45402-2241
Tel: 937-424-3391
Email: info@efwa.org
http://www.efwa.org

For free office career and salary information, visit
OfficeTeam
http://www.officeteam.com

Business Managers

OVERVIEW

Business managers plan, organize, direct, and coordinate the operations of firms in business and industry. They may oversee an entire company, a geographical territory of a company's operations, or a specific department within a company. Of the approximately 2.1 million managerial jobs in the United States, more than 75 percent are found in service-providing industries (including the government).

HISTORY

The term *manage* means to handle, direct, or control. Everyone has some experience in management. For example, if you schedule your day so that you can get up, get to school on time, go to soccer practice after school, have the time to do your homework, and get to bed at a reasonable hour, you are practicing management skills. Running a household, paying bills, balancing a checkbook, and keeping track of appointments, meetings, and social activities are also examples of managerial activities.

Management is a necessary part of any enterprise in which a person or group of people are trying to accomplish a specific goal. In fact, civilization could not have grown to its present level of complexity without the planning and organizing involved in effective management. Some of the earliest examples of written documents had to do with the management of business and commerce. As societies and individuals accumulated property and wealth, they needed effective record keeping of taxes, trade agreements, laws, and rights of ownership.

The technological advances of the industrial revolution brought about the need for a distinct class of managers. As complex factory systems developed, skilled and trained managers were required to organize and operate them. Workers became specialized in a limited number of tasks, which required managers to coordinate and oversee production.

As businesses began to diversify their production, industries became so complex that their management had to be divided among several different managers, as opposed to one central manager. With the expanded scope of managers and the trend toward decentralized management, the transition to the professional manager took place. In the 1920s, large corporations began to organize with decentralized administration and centralized policy control.

Managers provided a forum for the exchange and evaluation of creative ideas and technical innovations. Eventually these management concepts spread from manufacturing and production to office, personnel, marketing, and financial functions. Today, management is more concerned with results than activities, taking into account individual differences in styles of working.

THE JOB

Management is found in every industry, including food, clothing, banking, education, health care, and business services. All types of businesses have managers to formulate policies and administer the firm's operations. Managers may oversee the operations of an entire company, a geographical territory of a company's operations, or a specific department, such as sales and marketing.

Business managers direct a company's or a department's daily activities within the context of the organization's overall plan. They implement organizational policies and goals. This may involve developing sales or promotional materials, analyzing the department's budgetary requirements, and hiring, training, and supervising staff. Business managers are often responsible for long-range planning for their company or department. This involves setting goals for the organization and developing a workable plan for meeting those goals.

A manager responsible for a single department might work to coordinate his or her department's activities with other departments. A manager responsible for an entire company or organization might work with the managers of various departments or locations to oversee and coordinate the activities of all departments. If the business is privately owned, the owner may be the manager. In a large

The president (*left*) of a leasing agency talks with a payroll administrator. (*Syracuse Newspapers/The Image Works*)

corporation, however, there will be a management structure above the business manager.

Jeff Bowe is the Midwest general manager for Disc Graphics, a large printing company headquartered in New York. Bowe oversees all aspects of the company's Indianapolis plant, which employs about 50 people. When asked what he is responsible for, Bowe answers, "Everything that happens in this facility." Specifically, that includes sales, production, customer service, capital expenditure planning, hiring and training employees, firing or downsizing, and personnel management.

The hierarchy of managers includes top executives, such as the president, who establishes an organization's goals and policies along with others, such as the chief executive officer, chief financial officer, chief information officer, executive vice president, and the board of directors. Top executives plan business objectives and develop policies to coordinate operations between divisions and departments and establish procedures for attaining objectives. Activity reports and financial statements are reviewed to determine progress and revise operations as needed. The president also directs and formulates funding for new and existing programs within the organization. Public relations plays a big part in the lives of executives as they deal with executives and leaders from other countries or organizations, and with customers, employees, and various special interest groups.

The top-level managers for Bowe's company are located in the company's New York headquarters. Bowe is responsible for reporting certain information about the Indianapolis facility to them. He may also have to work collaboratively with them on certain projects or plans. "I have a conversation with people at headquarters about every two to three days," he says. "I get corporate input on very large projects. I would also work closely with them if we had some type of corporate-wide program we were working on—something where I would be the contact person for this facility."

Although the president or chief executive officer retains ultimate authority and responsibility, Bowe is responsible for overseeing the day-to-day operations of the Indianapolis location. A manager in this position is sometimes called a *chief operating officer* or COO. Other duties of a COO may include serving as chairman of committees, such as those for management, executive, engineering, or sales.

Some companies have an *executive vice president,* who directs and coordinates the activities of one or more departments, depending on the size of the organization. In very large organizations, the duties of executive vice presidents may be highly specialized. For example, they may oversee the activities of business managers of marketing, sales promotion, purchasing, finance, personnel training, industrial relations, administrative services, data processing, property management, transportation, or legal services. In smaller organizations, an executive vice president may be responsible for a number of these departments. Executive vice presidents also assist the chief executive officer in formulating and administering the organization's policies and developing its long-range goals. Executive vice presidents may serve as members of management committees on special studies.

Companies may also have a *chief financial officer* or CFO. In small firms, the CFO is usually responsible for all financial management tasks, such as budgeting, capital expenditure planning, cash flow, and various financial reviews and reports. In larger companies, the CFO may oversee financial management departments, to help other managers develop financial and economic policy and oversee the implementation of these policies.

Chief information officers, or *CIOs,* are responsible for all aspects of their company's information technology. They use their knowledge of technology and business to determine how information technology can best be used to meet company goals. This may include researching, purchasing, and overseeing the set up and use of technology systems, such as intranet, Internet, and computer networks. These managers sometimes take a role in implementing a company's Web site.

In companies that have several different locations, managers may be assigned to oversee specific geographic areas. For example, a large retailer with facilities all across the nation is likely to have a number of managers in charge of various territories. There might be a Midwest manager, a Southwest manager, a Southeast manager, a Northeast manager, and a Northwest manager. These managers are often called *regional* or *area managers*. Some companies break their management territories up into even smaller sections, such as a single state or a part of a state. Managers overseeing these smaller segments are often called *district managers,* and typically report directly to an area or regional manager.

REQUIREMENTS

High School
The educational background of business managers varies as widely as the nature of their diverse responsibilities. Many have a bachelor's degree in liberal arts or business administration. If you are interested in a business managerial career, you should start preparing in high school by taking college preparatory classes. According to Jeff Bowe, your best bet academically is to get a well-rounded education. Because communication is important, take as many English classes as possible. Speech classes are another way to improve your communication skills. Courses in mathematics, business, and computer science are also excellent choices to help you prepare for this career. Finally, Bowe recommends taking a foreign language. "Today speaking a foreign language is more and more important," he says. "Which language is not so important. Any of the global languages are something you could very well use, depending upon where you end up."

Postsecondary Training
Business managers often have a college degree in a subject that pertains to the department they direct or the organization they administer; for example, accounting or economics for a business manager of finance, computer science for a business manager of data processing, engineering or science for a director of research and development. As computer usage grows, managers are expected to have experience with the information technology that applies to their field.

Graduate and professional degrees are common. Bowe, along with many managers in administrative, marketing, financial, and manufacturing activities, has a master of business administration. Managers in highly technical manufacturing and research activities often have either a master's degree or a doctorate in a technical or scientific discipline. A law degree is mandatory for business managers of corporate legal departments, and hospital managers generally have a master's degree in health services administration or business administration. In some industries, such as retail trade or the food and beverage industry, competent individuals without a college degree may become business managers.

Other Requirements

There are a number of personal characteristics that can help one become a successful business manager. A manager who oversees other employees should have good communication and interpersonal skills. The ability to delegate work is another important personality trait of a good manager. The ability to think on your feet is often key in business management, according to Bowe. "You have to be able to think extremely quickly and not in a reactionary manner," he says. Bowe also says that a certain degree of organization is important, since managers often juggle several different tasks simultaneously. Other traits considered important for top executives are intelligence, decisiveness, intuition, creativity, honesty, loyalty, and a sense of responsibility. Finally, the successful manager should be flexible and interested in staying abreast of new developments in his or her industry. "In general, you need to be open to change because your customers change, your market changes, your technology changes," he says. "If you won't try something new, you really have no business being in management."

EXPLORING

To get experience as a manager, start looking for opportunities within your areas of interest. Whether you're involved in drama, sports, school publications, or a part-time job, there are managerial duties associated with any organized activity. These can involve planning, scheduling, fund-raising, budgeting, or managing other workers or volunteers. Local businesses also have job opportunities through which you can get firsthand knowledge and experience of management structure. If you can't get an actual job, try to at least schedule a meeting with a business manager to talk with him or her about the career. Some schools or community organizations arrange job-shadowing, where you can spend part of a day "shadowing" a selected employee to see what his or her job is like. Joining Junior Achievement (http://www.ja.org) is another excellent way to get involved with local businesses and learn about how they work. Finally, take every opportunity to work with computers, since computer skills are vital to today's business world.

EMPLOYERS

There are approximately 2.1 million general and operations managers and executives employed in the United States. These jobs are found in every industry. However, approximately 75 percent work in service industries.

Virtually every business in the United States has some form of managerial position. Obviously, the larger the company is, the more managerial positions it is likely to have. Another factor is the geographical territory covered by the business. It is safe to say that companies doing business in larger geographical territories are likely to have more managerial positions than those within smaller territories.

STARTING OUT

Generally you will need a college degree, although many retail stores, grocery stores, and restaurants hire promising applicants who have only a high school diploma. Job seekers usually apply directly to the manager of such places. Your college career services office is often the best place to start looking for these positions. A number of listings can also be found in newspaper help wanted ads.

Many organizations have management trainee programs that college graduates can enter. Such programs are advertised at college career fairs or through college job placement services. Often, however, these management trainee positions in business and government are filled by employees who are already working for the organization and who demonstrate management potential. Jeff Bowe suggests researching the industry you are interested in to find out what might be the best point of entry for that field. "I came into the printing company through customer service, which is a good point of entry because it's one of the easiest things to learn," he says. "Although it requires more technical know-how now than it did then, customer service is still not a bad entry point for this industry."

ADVANCEMENT

Most business management and top executive positions are filled through the promotion of experienced lower-level managers and executives who display valuable managerial traits, such as leadership, self-confidence, creativity, motivation, decisiveness, and flexibility. In small firms advancement to a higher management position may come slowly, while promotions may occur more quickly in larger firms.

Participating in different kinds of educational programs available for managers may accelerate advancement in this career. These programs are often paid for by the organization. Company training programs broaden knowledge of company policy and operations. Training programs sponsored by industry and trade associations and continuing education courses in colleges and universities can familiarize managers with the latest developments in management techniques.

In recent years, large numbers of middle managers were laid off as companies streamlined operations. Competition for jobs is keen, and business managers committed to improving their knowledge of the field and of related disciplines—especially computer information systems—will have the best opportunities for advancement.

Business managers may advance to executive or administrative vice president. Vice presidents may advance to peak corporate positions—president or chief executive officer. Presidents and chief executive officers, upon retirement, may become members of the board of directors of one or more firms. Sometimes business managers establish their own firms.

EARNINGS

Salary levels for business managers vary substantially, depending upon the level of responsibility, length of service, and type, size, and location of the organization. Top-level managers in large firms can earn much more than their counterparts in small firms. Also, salaries in large metropolitan areas such as New York City are higher than those in smaller cities.

According to the U.S. Department of Labor, general and operations managers had a median yearly income of $88,700 in 2007. To show the range of earnings for general and operations managers, however, the department notes that those in the computer and peripheral equipment manufacturing industry had a mean salary of $150,990; those in Internet publishing and broadcasting, $147,030; and those employed in local government, $83,550.

Chief executives earned a mean annual salary of $151,370 in 2007, according to the U.S. Department of Labor. Ten percent of chief executives earned less than $64,530. Again, salaries varied by industry. For example, the mean yearly salary for those involved in the management of companies and enterprises was $174,560, while those employed by depository credit intermediation companies earned a mean of $155,760. The business publication *The NonProfit Times,* which conducts periodic salary surveys, reports the average yearly earnings for CEOs and executive directors at nonprofit social services and welfare organizations were approximately $100,118 in 2006. Some executives, however, have annual salaries that are hundreds of thousands of dollars more than the figures listed here.

Benefit and compensation packages for business managers are usually excellent, and may even include such things as bonuses, stock awards, company-paid insurance premiums, use of company cars, paid country club memberships, expense accounts, and generous retirement benefits.

WORK ENVIRONMENT

Business managers are provided with comfortable offices near the departments they direct. Top executives may have spacious, lavish offices and may enjoy such privileges as executive dining rooms, company cars, country club memberships, and liberal expense accounts.

Managers often travel between national, regional, and local offices. Top executives may travel to meet with executives in other corporations, both within the United States and abroad. Meetings and conferences sponsored by industries and associations occur regularly and provide invaluable opportunities to meet with peers and keep up with the latest developments. In large corporations, job transfers between the parent company and its local offices or subsidiaries are common.

Business managers often work long hours under intense pressure to meet the company's production and marketing goals. Jeff Bowe's average workweek consists of 55 to 60 hours at the office. This is not uncommon—in fact, some executive spend up to 80 hours working each week. These long hours limit time available for family and leisure activities.

OUTLOOK

Overall, employment of business managers and executives is expected to experience little or no growth through 2016, according to the U.S. Department of Labor. Many job openings will be the result of managers being promoted to better positions, retiring, or leaving their positions to start their own businesses. Even so, the compensation and prestige of these positions make them highly sought-after, and competition to fill openings will be intense.

Projected employment growth varies by industry. For example, employment in the professional, scientific, and technical services industry should increase faster than the average, while employment in some manufacturing industries is expected to decline. Job opportunities in administrative and support services are expected to grow about as fast as the average.

The outlook for business managers is closely tied to the overall economy. When the economy is good, businesses expand both in terms of their output and the number of people they employ, which creates a need for more managers. In economic downturns, businesses often lay off employees and cut back on production, which lessens the need for managers.

Business managers who have knowledge of one or more foreign languages (such as Spanish or Mandarin) and experience in marketing, international economics, and information systems will have the best employment opportunities.

FOR MORE INFORMATION

For news about management trends, resources on career information and finding a job, and an online job bank, contact
American Management Association
1601 Broadway
New York, NY 10019-7434
Tel: 877-566-9441
http://www.amanet.org

For information about programs for students in kindergarten through high school, and information on local chapters, contact
Junior Achievement
One Education Way
Colorado Springs, CO 80906-4477
Tel: 719-540-8000
Email: newmedia@ja.org
http://www.ja.org

For information on management careers, contact
National Management Association
2210 Arbor Boulevard
Dayton, OH 45439-1506
Tel: 937-294-0421
Email: nma@nma1.org
http://nma1.org

INTERVIEW

Margaret Nightengale is a senior vice president at Grant County Bank in Ulysses, Kansas. She discussed her career with the editors of Careers in Focus: Business.

Q. Why did you decide to pursue a career in banking?

A. I happened into my banking career by accident. I was looking for something in my local community that would utilize my accounting degree. I happened to run into the bank president one afternoon and we discussed a potential opening at the bank for an internal auditor. Luckily, I followed up on the lead and have been happily employed at the bank for the past 12 years.

Q. Can you please take us through a day in your life as a senior vice president? What are your typical tasks/ responsibilities?

A. My main responsibilities are as a commercial and agriculture loan officer. In our bank, our loan officers perform the credit analysis and make recommendations on which loans we should approve and why. Our loan committee meets as often as necessary to review pending requests. The lending process does not stop once the decision has been made and the customer signs the documents. Ongoing monitoring of the line and the customer are required to determine if conditions exist that jeopardize the collectability of the loan. Unfortunately, there are times when the customer is not able to meet the original obligations of the loan. Foreclosure or collection activity must then be initiated, and the best possible course of action must be determined.

In addition to being a loan officer, I also serve on our executive committee. This committee is made up of other senior level officers in the bank and collectively is labeled "management." We review all areas of bank performance and make decisions on macro-level issues.

I supervise the marketing function and the compliance function of the bank as well. Both are ancillary support functions that are absolutely necessary to the smooth, ongoing operations of the bank. Compliance with federal and state regulatory issues is a must if the bank wishes to keep its doors open. We are examined on a routine basis by several regulatory bodies.

In the same way, marketing to our existing and potential customer base is necessary to determine if the products and services we offer are meeting our customer's needs. Knowing the market in which you operate is essential to ongoing profitability and providing excellent customer service.

Q. What do you like most and least about your job?

A. One of the areas that I find to be the most challenging is supervision of people. Dealing with issues that arise with personnel is a delicate skill. It is also one that is not easily learned from reading a book or attending a class or workshop. Every situation with every employee must be well thought out and planned based upon that person's life experiences, personality, and skill set. Effectively dealing with confrontation and finding a way to provide a positive spin with employees is difficult, yet essential to the ongoing communication and ability to work together that is necessary in a work environment.

I have the distinct opportunity to get to work closely with people (customers and coworkers), as well as tap my natural ability to work with numbers. Analyzing numbers and assisting my customers in making better business decisions is one of my favorite aspects of my job.

Q. What advice would you give to high school students who are interested in this career?

A. Take full advantage of the opportunities to learn as much as your brain can absorb. You will quickly understand that learning and education do not stop after high school or college. Professionals must continually expand their knowledge base to succeed in today's marketplace.

Also, take every opportunity to study and understand people. Relationships with your family, friends, and coworkers will help be the deciding element to your success. You cannot succeed without support and love from others.

Set realistic, achievable, and measurable goals for yourself. Having earned the respect of your coworkers is much more valuable than friendship. Conduct yourself with the highest amounts of ethics and integrity, every time, every day.

Q. What are the most important professional qualities for financial officers and managers?

A. Confidentiality and respect of your customers and their [personal] information has to be at the top of the list. Treating their business and information with the utmost care and respect conveys the message that they are valued customers of the bank and their trust and confidence is very important. Customers who don't trust you won't be straight with you when the times are tough and they are squeezed.

It remains without saying that solid ethics and high moral standards are essential to a successful career. Unfortunately, at some point in your life, you will be asked to do something that makes you uncomfortable. Follow your gut and your heart. Stand up for your beliefs. The short-term implications may be devastating, but the long-term impact will be worth it.

Good time management skills are also important. The multiple demands of your career, family life, and community schedule are very trying and exhausting. Use your personal, family, and careers goals to help you set your priorities. You will have to learn to say "no" to projects, groups, organizations, and kids in order to keep balanced and focused.

Chief Information Officers

OVERVIEW

Chief information officers (CIOs), also known as *information systems directors,* are responsible for all aspects of their company's information technology. They use their knowledge of technology and business to determine how information technology can best be used to meet company goals. This may include researching, purchasing, and overseeing the set-up and use of technology systems, such as intranet, Internet, and computer networks. These managers sometimes take a role in implementing a company's Web site. CIOs work for a variety of employers, including businesses, government agencies, libraries, and colleges and universities.

HISTORY

Over the past few decades, the importance of computer technology and the Internet has increased rapidly. The Internet, which did not exist in its current form until 1983, is now an integral part of nearly all business. It allows companies to conduct transactions in a matter of seconds, and people all over the world now rely on the World Wide Web as a quick resource on everything from education and current events to shopping and the stock market.

Because of this boom in the use and importance of computers and the Internet, workers must constantly be updated about changes in technology. It is the job of the chief information officer to make sure that all technology runs smoothly in an office, and that no workers are in the dark when it comes to the company's computer systems. The position of chief information officer, though a relatively new job title, has quickly risen in importance and prestige and is firmly established among the top executive positions available in the business world.

THE JOB

Anyone who has read Scott Adams' comic strip *Dilbert* knows something about the imaginary wall between business executives and technology experts in the corporate world. On one side of the wall (so the *Dilbert* story goes), there are the folks who wear business suits and who don't know a laptop from an Etch-A-Sketch. On the other side of the wall, there are the geeks in tennis shoes who hang out in *Battlestar Galactica* chat rooms and couldn't care less about the company's mission statement. If popular lore is to be believed, confusion, hostility, and poor business practices abound whenever these two groups try to join forces.

It's the job of the CIO to enter this ongoing battle and find a way to straddle the wall between business and technology. Although they're up to date on cutting-edge information technology, today's CIOs must know their way around the company's business as well as any other high-level manager. That means they attend strategy sessions and management meetings in addition to meeting with computer professionals and other members of the technical staff. Using their combined business and technical know-how, CIOs usually oversee the selection and implementation of their company's information systems—from email programs to corporation-wide intranets.

Making these decisions requires enough technical savvy to choose appropriate technology systems from an array of options. Decisions like these, though, also require a sophisticated sense of how information in a company circulates and how that information relates to business practices. Does the company's customer database need to connect to the World Wide Web? What security issues are created if that connection is established? Who needs to be able to access the most sensitive information, and who needs to be locked out? Answering these sorts of questions can take all of a CIO's mix of executive knowledge and technical expertise.

For Chuck Cooper, the director of information systems at a major public library, making these sorts of decisions also requires a good understanding of the financial situation of his organization. He must select systems for his library staff that fit their needs and the library's often-limited budget. At the same time, he must consider what the library may need five or even 10 years down the road, since a lack of vision now could mean more money and time spent later. After systems have been selected, Cooper must establish and oversee vendor relationships (contractual agreements between the library and companies that supply technical equipment). Evaluating potential vendor relationships for financial and technological advantages takes up a large part of the CIO's working hours.

For most CIOs, however, choosing and implementing technology systems is just the beginning. For example, Cooper spends much of his time keeping employees informed and enthusiastic about new computer technology. "I spend a lot of my time trying to convince people of the utility of new systems," he explains. "Library people are reality-oriented. They have to kick the tires." For Cooper, giving his employees a chance to "kick the tires" of new systems means organizing targeted, hands-on demonstration sessions. Once they have a chance to test-drive new programs themselves, employees often become excited about the new services they'll be able to provide to library patrons.

REQUIREMENTS

High School
If you are interested in this career, you should start preparing in high school by taking college preparatory classes. Take as many computer science, mathematics, business, and English classes as possible. Speech classes are another way to improve your communication skills.

Postsecondary Training
Becoming a CIO requires a solid technology background and solid business understanding. In general, companies require their executives to have at least a bachelor of arts or bachelor of science degree, and often a master of business administration as well.

If you're interested in becoming a CIO, you should be sure that your college degree provides you with both business and computer skills. Some programs devoted to providing this sort of background have begun to spring up, such as those offered by the School of Information at the University of California, Berkeley (http://www.ischool.berkeley.edu/programs/overview). The school offers a master's and a Ph.D. in information management and systems.

Other Requirements
Equally important to training, though, are the communication skills you'll need to sell your coworkers and staff on the information strat-

egies that you build. "Writing and especially speaking are crucial in this business," Chuck Cooper points out. "You are constantly presenting yourself and your work to others, and you need to be able to communicate well in order to succeed." English, writing, and speech classes should help you hone your verbal communication skills.

EXPLORING

The best way to explore this field while you are still in high school is by joining computer clubs at school and community centers and learning all you can about the Internet, networks, and computer security. You might also get a part-time job that includes computer work. This can help you get exposure to computer systems and how they are used in a business.

To get management experience, start with your own interests. There are managerial duties associated with almost every organized activity, from the drama club or theatrical productions to sports or school publications.

EMPLOYERS

Until fairly recently, CIOs were found primarily at large corporations that could afford another high-level executive salary. According to *Inc.* magazine, though, smaller companies are now beginning to see the value of having a dedicated information director. "At smaller companies, technology has often been placed too low in the organization," Chuck Cooper points out. Without executive decision-making power, technology professionals often found their recommendations given insufficient weight. While this sort of strategy may save money in the short-term, small companies have gradually discovered that they pay later when outdated systems must be upgraded or altered. In fact, even nonprofits and other less mainstream small businesses have begun to hire CIOs.

STARTING OUT

Since CIOs are high-level executives, people usually spend several years working in business administration or information management before they apply for jobs at the CIO level. Lower- and mid-level information management jobs usually involve specialization in a certain area. For example, middle-level systems management professionals in Chuck Cooper's department may run technology training programs, design and implement help desks, or oversee small database systems.

ADVANCEMENT

After they've proven themselves at lower-level information management jobs, these employees begin to manage larger units, such as the user support program or the larger library database system. Eventually, some of these employees may have the business experience and broad technical background required to apply for jobs at the CIO level.

Other CIOs may find work at the executive level after making what's known as a "lateral move"—a move from a position in one department to a position at the same level in another department. For example, successful business administration professionals might be able to move into an information systems department as a manager rather than an entry-level database administrator. But they would still need to prove they had managed to gain the technical know-how required to do the job.

EARNINGS

Earnings among CIOs vary substantially based on factors such as the type of business, the size of the employer, or the executive's experience. *Computerworld* reports that chief information officers earned an average salary (including bonuses) of $184,750 in 2008. According to the U.S. Department of Labor, the mean annual income for all top executives, which includes CIOs, was $151,370 in 2007. The business publication *The NonProfit Times,* which conducts periodic salary surveys, reports the average earnings for top executives at nonprofit social services and welfare organizations were approximately $100,118 in 2006. This shows that even those working for nonprofits command extremely high salaries.

Benefits for CIOs depend on the employer but generally include health insurance, retirement plans, and paid vacation and sick days. Bonuses and stock options may also be offered.

WORK ENVIRONMENT

For Chuck Cooper, the best part of being a CIO comes when new technology is put in place. "When you see the effect of probably a year of planning, and it has a positive impact on the way the public uses the library, that's a nice feeling," he remarks. Because CIOs often spend time thinking about changes that will be implemented several years down the road, having a program finally "hit the streets," as Cooper puts it, is gratifying, especially when it allows library patrons and staff to access information in a way they never could before.

Although the payoff can be gratifying, the planning may not be, Cooper admits. "There's a lot of frustration caused by dead ends," he explains. "There are often projects that you try to get started that are dependent on other people, and you may have to wait or start over." The interdependence between technology and other library areas means that Cooper often spends years revising plans before they can get the go-ahead. The need to take strategies back to the drawing board can be the worst part of Cooper's work.

OUTLOOK

According to the U.S. Department of Labor, top executives, including CIOs, should experience little or no employment growth through 2016. As consumers and industries increasingly rely on computers and information technology, the expertise of CIOs will be in continuous demand. As computer technology becomes more sophisticated and more complex, corporations will increasingly require information science professionals capable of choosing among the ever-growing array of information technology options. Additionally, as small organizations begin to prioritize information management, more jobs should be available for CIOs outside of large corporations. Because some of these jobs are likely to be at nonprofit and educational institutions, information science professionals may have wider options when choosing an employer. Although salaries can be expected to be lower at these sorts of organizations, they may provide interested employees with a less formal and more service-oriented atmosphere.

FOR MORE INFORMATION

To read about issues in the field, visit
  CIO.com
  http://www.cio.com

For information on careers, contact
  Information Technology Association of America
  1401 Wilson Boulevard, Suite 1100
  Arlington, VA 22209-2318
  Tel: 703-522-5055
  http://www.itaa.org

For information about programs for students in kindergarten through high school, and information on local chapters, contact
  Junior Achievement
  One Education Way

Colorado Springs, CO 80906-4477
Tel: 719-540-8000
Email: newmedia@ja.org
http://www.ja.org

For information on career opportunities in state government, contact
National Association of State Chief Information Officers
c/o AMR Management Services
201 East Main Street, Suite 1405
Lexington, KY 40507-2004
http://www.nascio.org

Cultural Advisers

OVERVIEW

Cultural advisers, also known as *bilingual consultants*, work with businesses and organizations to help them communicate effectively with people who are from different cultural and linguistic backgrounds. Cultural advisers usually have a specialty such as business management, banking, education, or computer technology. They help bridge both language and cultural barriers in our increasingly global business world.

HISTORY

Communication has always been a challenge when cultures come into contact with each other. In the early days of the United States, settlers and explorers relied on interpreters to assist them. One of those famous interpreters, Sacajawea, a member of the Shoshone Indian tribe, was a precursor of the cultural advisers of today. As she helped guide Meriwether Lewis and William Clark across the West to the Pacific Ocean, she acted as interpreter when they encountered Native American tribes. She also helped the explorers adapt to different cultures and customs.

Today's cultural advisers work with companies or organizations that need to communicate effectively and do business with other cultures. Cultural advisers are becoming even more valuable because it is now relatively quick and easy to travel throughout the world. Each year, more trade barriers are broken down by legislation, such as the North American Free Trade Agreement, implemented in 1994.

THE JOB

Cultural advisers work to bridge gaps in communication and culture. They usually have a second specialty that is complemented by their bilingual skills. For example, a banking and finance expert who has traveled extensively in Japan and is familiar with Japanese language and customs would have the marketable skills to become a cultural adviser for American companies interested in doing business in Japan.

Cultural advisers work in a wide variety of settings. They may hold full-time staff positions with organizations or they may work as independent consultants providing services to a number of clients. Cultural advisers may also work in education. In this capacity they might provide translation services and help foreign or immigrant students adjust to a new culture. They might also educate teachers and administrators to make them aware of cultural differences, so that programs and classes can be adapted to include everyone. Colleges and universities that have large international student populations often have cultural advisers on staff.

In industry, cultural advisers train workers in safety procedures and worker rights. The health care industry benefits from the use of advisers to communicate with non-English-speaking patients. Cultural advisers also hold training sessions for health care professionals to teach them how to better understand and instruct their patients.

Large business enterprises that have overseas interests hire cultural advisers to research new markets and help with negotiations. Some advisers work primarily in employment, finding foreign experts to work for American businesses or finding overseas jobs for American workers. In addition to advising American business leaders, cultural advisers sometimes work with foreign entities that want to do business in the United States. They provide English language instruction and training in American business practices.

Cultural advisers also work in advertising, social services, government agencies, the legal system, the media, and the travel industry. Whatever the setting, cultural advisers help their clients—foreign and domestic—understand and respect other cultures and communicate effectively with them.

REQUIREMENTS

High School

Classes in business, speech, and foreign language will give you an excellent head start to becoming a cultural adviser. In addition, take other classes in your high school's college-prep curriculum. These courses should include history, mathematics, sciences, and English.

Accounting classes and computer science classes will also help prepare you for working in business.

Postsecondary Training
If you are planning a career as a cultural adviser, fluency in two or more languages is a requirement; thus, you should probably major or minor in a foreign language in college. Courses in business, world history, world geography, and sociology would be useful as well. You will need at least a bachelor's degree to find work as a cultural adviser, and you may want to consider pursuing a master's degree to have more job opportunities. Many universities offer programs in cultural studies, and there are master's programs that offer a concentration in international business.

Take advantage of every opportunity to learn about the people and area you want to work with. Studying abroad for a semester or year is also recommended.

Other Requirements
Cultural sensitivity is the number-one requirement for an adviser. Knowing the history, culture, and social conventions of a people in addition to their language is a very important part of the job. Also, expertise in another area, such as business, education, law, or computers, is necessary to be a cultural adviser.

EXPLORING
A good way to explore this field is to join one of your high school's foreign language clubs. In addition to using the foreign language, these clubs often have activities related to the culture where the language is spoken. You may also find it helpful to join your school's business club, which will give you an opportunity to learn about business tactics and finances, as well as give you an idea of how to run your own business.

Learn as much as you can about people and life in other parts of the world. You can do this by joining groups such as American Field Service (AFS) and getting to know a student from another country who is attending your school. There are also study and living abroad programs that you can apply to even while in high school. Rotary International and AFS offer such opportunities; see the end of this article for contact information.

EMPLOYERS
Cultural advisers are employed on a contract or project basis by businesses, associations, and educational institutions. Large global

Most Popular Foreign Languages Studied by College Students

Cultural advisers typically have knowledge of at least one other language than English. Here were the most popular modern foreign languages studied at U.S. colleges and universities in 2006:

Language	Enrollment	Increase Since 2002
1. Spanish	822,985	+10.3 percent
2. French	206,426	+2.2 percent
3. German	94,264	+3.5 percent
4. Italian	78,368	+22.6 percent
5. Japanese	66,605	+27.5 percent
6. Chinese	51,582	+51.0 percent
7. Russian	24,845	+3.9 percent
8. Arabic	23,974	+126.5 percent
9. Portuguese	10,267	+22.4 percent
10. Modern Hebrew	9,612	+11.5 percent

Source: *Enrollments in Languages Other Than English in United States Institutions of Higher Education, Fall 2006*, Modern Language Association of America

companies are the most significant source of employment for cultural advisers as they seek to serve the global population. Small to medium-sized companies that do business in a particular region also employ cultural advisers. Companies in large cities offer the most opportunities for cultural advisers, especially those cities that border other countries.

Miguel Orta is a cultural adviser in North Miami Beach, Florida. He works with Latin American companies and American companies doing business in Central America and South America. He also has a background in law and business management. Orta is fluent in English, Spanish, and Portuguese. He uses his location in Florida to help businesses in the United States interact with the country's growing Hispanic population. His Florida location also allows him to be only a short plane flight from his Latin American clients.

STARTING OUT

Most cultural advisers do not begin this career right after college. Some real-life experience is necessary to be qualified to fill the cultural adviser's role. "Education is very important," says Miguel Orta. "But first you need some work in the trenches." Once that experience is obtained, you will be ready to try advising.

After graduating with a law degree, Orta spent several years as a private attorney representing many Latin American clients. He practiced corporate, international, and labor law. When the opportunity came to serve one of his Venezuelan clients as a cultural adviser, Orta enjoyed the work and decided to become an adviser to others in need of those services.

ADVANCEMENT

Working with larger companies on more extensive projects is one way for a cultural adviser to advance. If an adviser decides to trade in the flexibility and freedom of working on projects independently, opportunities to become a salaried employee would most likely be available.

EARNINGS

Cultural advisers are well compensated for the time they spend on projects. Rates can range from approximately $65 to as high as $265 per hour. The median rate is close to $100 per hour. Advisers may incur business expenses, but their clients generally pay many of the expenses associated with the work, such as travel, meals, and lodging.

WORK ENVIRONMENT

The work environment of cultural advisers depends largely on their specialties. A smaller company may offer a more informal setting than a multinational corporation. A cultural adviser who is employed by a large, international bank may travel much more than an adviser who works for an educational institution or association.

While cultural advisers generally work independently on projects, they must also communicate with a large number of people to complete their tasks. In the middle of a project, a cultural adviser may work 50 to 60 hours per week and travel may be necessary. Between projects, cultural advisers manage their businesses and solicit new clients.

OUTLOOK

The field of cultural advising is predicted to grow faster than the average for all careers in the next decade. Demand will grow as trade barriers are continually loosened and U.S. companies conduct more business on a global scale. Latin America and Asia are two promising areas for American businesses.

Cultural advisers will also be needed to address the interests of the increasingly diverse population of the United States. However, competition is keen, and those with graduate degrees and specific expertise will be the most successful.

FOR MORE INFORMATION

For information about cultural exchanges, contact the AFS and Rotary International.

American Field Service (AFS)
71 West 23rd Street, 17th Floor
New York, NY 10010-4183
Tel: 212-352-9810
Email: info.center@afs.org
http://www.afs.org

Rotary International
One Rotary Center
1560 Sherman Avenue
Evanston, IL 60201-4818
Tel: 847-866-3000
http://www.rotary.org

For information on etiquette and cross-cultural training, contact
Protocol Advisors Inc.
35 Pinckney Street
Boston, MA 02114-4801
Tel: 617-227-2220
Email: info@protocoladvisors.com
http://www.protocoladvisors.com

Customer Service Representatives

OVERVIEW

Customer service representatives, sometimes called *customer care representatives*, work with customers of one or many companies, assist with customer problems, or answer questions. Customer service representatives work in many different industries to provide "front-line" customer service in a variety of businesses. Most customer service representatives work in an office setting, though some may work in the "field" to better meet customer needs. There are approximately 2.2 million customer service representatives employed in the United States.

HISTORY

Customer service has been a part of business for many years; however, the formal title of customer service representative is relatively new. In 1988, the International Customer Service Association established Customer Service Week to recognize and promote customer service.

As the world moves toward a more global and competitive economic market, customer service, along with quality control, has taken a front seat in the business world. Serving customers and serving them well is more important now than ever before.

Customer service is about communication, so the progress in customer service can be tied closely to the progress in the communication industry. When Alexander Graham Bell invented the telephone in 1876, he probably did not envision the customer service lines, automated response messages, toll-free phone numbers, and computer technology that now help customer service representatives do their jobs.

The increased use of the Internet has helped companies serve and communicate with their customers in another way. From the simple email complaint form to online help files, companies are using the Internet to provide better customer service. Some companies even have online chat capabilities to communicate with their customers instantaneously via the Web.

THE JOB

Julie Cox is a customer service representative for Affina. Affina is a call center that handles customer service for a variety of companies. Cox works with each of Affina's clients and the call center operators to ensure that each call-in receives top customer service. Customer service representatives often handle complaints and problems, and Cox finds that to be the case at the call center as well. While the operators who report to her provide customer service to those on the phone, Cox must oversee that customer service while also keeping in mind the customer service for her clients, whatever business they may be in.

"I make sure that the clients get regular reports of the customer service calls and check to see if there are any recurring problems," says Cox.

One of the ways Cox observes if customer service is not being handled effectively is by monitoring the actual time spent on each phone call. If an operator spends a lot of time on a call, there is most likely a problem.

"Our customers are billed per minute," says Cox. "So we want to make sure their customer service is being handled well and efficiently."

Affina's call center in Columbus, Indiana, handles dozens of toll-free lines. While some calls are likely to be focused on complaints or questions, some are easier to handle. Cox and her staff handle calls from people simply wanting to order literature, brochures, or to find the nearest dealer location.

Customer service representatives work in a variety of fields and business, but one thing is common—the customer. All businesses depend on their customers to keep them in business, so customer service, whether handled internally or outsourced to a call center like Affina, is extremely important.

Some customer service representatives, like Cox, do most of their work on the telephone. Others may represent companies in the field, where the customer is actually using the product or service. Still other customer service representatives may specialize in Internet

Successful customer service representatives must enjoy working with people and assisting them with their questions and problems. *(Rob Lewine/Corbis)*

service, assisting customers over the World Wide Web via email or online chats.

Affina's call center is available to their clients 24 hours a day, seven days a week, so Cox and her staff must keep around-the-clock shifts.

Not all customer service representatives work a varied schedule; many work a traditional daytime shift. However, customers have problems, complaints, and questions 24 hours a day, so many companies do staff their customer service positions for a longer number of hours, especially to accommodate customers during evenings and weekends.

REQUIREMENTS

High School

A high school diploma is required for most customer service representative positions. High school courses that emphasize communication, such as English and speech, will help you learn to communicate clearly. Any courses that require collaboration with others will also help to teach diplomacy and tact—two important aspects of customer service. Business courses will help you get a good overview of the business world, one that is dependent on customers and customer service. Computer skills are also very important.

Postsecondary Training

While a college degree is not necessary to become a customer service representative, certain areas of postsecondary training are helpful. Courses in business and organizational leadership will help to give you a better feel for the business world. Just as in high school, communications classes are helpful in learning to effectively talk with and meet the needs of other people.

These courses can be taken during a college curriculum or may be offered at a variety of customer service workshops or classes.

Read More About It

Evenson, Renee. *Customer Service Training 101: Quick and Easy Techniques That Get Great Results*. New York: AMACOM Books, 2005.

Karr, Ron, and Don Blohowiak. *The Complete Idiot's Guide to Great Customer Service*. New York: Alpha, 2003.

Knapp, Donna. *Guide to Customer Service Skills for the Help Desk Professional*. 3d ed. Boston: Course Technology, 2009.

Performance Research Associates. *Delivering Knock Your Socks Off Service*. 4th ed. New York: AMACOM Books, 2006.

Ukens, Lorraine L. *101 Ways to Improve Customer Service: Training, Tools, Tips, and Techniques*. Hoboken, N.J.: Pfeiffer, 2007.

Julie Cox is working as a customer service representative while she earns her business degree from a local college. Along with her college work, she has taken advantage of seminars and workshops to improve her customer service skills.

Bachelor's degrees in business and communications are increasingly required for managerial positions.

Certification or Licensing

Although it is not a requirement, customer service representatives can become certified. The International Customer Service Association and HDI offer certification to customer service professionals. Contact these organizations, listed at the end of this article, for more information.

Other Requirements

"The best and the worst parts of being a customer service representative are the people," Julie Cox says. Customer service representatives should have the ability to maintain a pleasant attitude at all times, even while serving angry or demanding customers.

A successful customer service representative will most likely have an outgoing personality and enjoy working with people and assisting them with their questions and problems.

Because many customer service representatives work in offices and on the telephone, people with physical disabilities may find this career to be both accessible and enjoyable.

EXPLORING

Julie Cox first discovered her love for customer service while working in retail at a local department store. Explore your ability for customer service by getting a job that deals with the public on a day-to-day basis. Talk with people who work with customers and customer service every day; find out what they like and dislike about their jobs.

There are other ways that you can prepare for a career in this field while you are still in school. Join your school's business club to get a feel for what goes on in the business world today. Doing volunteer work for a local charity or homeless shelter can help you decide if serving others is something that you'd enjoy doing as a career.

Evaluate the customer service at the businesses you visit. What makes that salesperson at The Gap better than the operator you talked with last week? Volunteer to answer phones at an agency in your town or city. Most receptionists in small companies and agencies are called on to provide customer service to callers. Try a nonprofit organization. They will welcome the help, and you will get a firsthand look at customer service.

EMPLOYERS

Customer service representatives are hired at all types of companies in a variety of areas. Industries that employ large numbers of customer service representatives include administrative and support services; retail trade establishments such as general merchandise stores and food and beverage stores; manufacturing, such as printing and related support activities; information, particularly the telecommunications industry; and wholesale trade. Because all businesses rely on customers, customer service is generally a high priority for those businesses. Some companies, like call centers, may employ a large number of customer service representatives to serve a multitude of clients, while small businesses may simply have one or two people who are responsible for customer service.

Approximately 30 percent of customer service representatives are employed in four states (California, Texas, Florida, and New York), but opportunities are available throughout the United States. In the United States, approximately 2.2 million workers are employed as customer service representatives.

STARTING OUT

You can become a customer service representative as an entry-level applicant, although some customer service representatives first serve in other areas of a company. This company experience may provide them with more knowledge and experience to answer customer questions. A college degree is not required, but any postsecondary training will increase your ability to find a job in customer service.

Ads for customer service job openings are readily available in newspapers and on Internet job search sites. With some experience and a positive attitude, it is possible to move into the position of customer service representative from another job within the company. Julie Cox started out at Affina as an operator and quickly moved into a customer service capacity.

ADVANCEMENT

Customer service experience is valuable in any business career path. Julie Cox hopes to combine her customer service experience with a business degree and move into the human resources area of the company.

It is also possible to advance to management or marketing jobs after working as a customer service representative. Businesses and their customers are inseparable, so most business professionals are experts at customer relations.

EARNINGS

Earnings vary based on location, level of experience, and size and type of employer. The U.S. Department of Labor reports the median annual income for all customer service representatives as $29,040 in 2007. Salaries ranged from less than $18,490 to more than $47,220. The Association of Support Professionals, which conducts salary surveys of tech support workers at software companies, reports that customer service representatives earned a median annual wage of $32,000 in 2007.

Other benefits vary widely according to the size and type of company in which representatives are employed. Benefits may include medical, dental, vision, and life insurance, 401(k) plans, or bonus incentives. Full-time customer service representatives can expect to receive vacation and sick pay, while part-time workers may not be offered these benefits.

WORK ENVIRONMENT

Customer service representatives work primarily indoors, although some may work in the field where the customers are using the product or service. They usually work in a supervised setting and report to a manager. They may spend many hours on the telephone, answering mail, or handling Internet communications. Many of the work hours involve little physical activity.

While most customer service representatives generally work a 40-hour workweek, others work a variety of shifts. Many businesses want customer service hours to coincide with the times that their customers are available to call or contact the business. For many companies, these times are in the evenings and on the weekends, so some customer service representatives work a varied shift and odd hours.

OUTLOOK

The U.S. Department of Labor predicts that employment for customer service representatives will grow much faster than the average for all occupations through 2016. This is a large field of workers and many replacement workers are needed each year as customer service reps leave this job for other positions, retire, or leave for other reasons. In addition, the Internet and e-commerce should increase the need for customer service representatives who will be needed to help customers navigate Web sites, answer questions over the phone, and respond to emails. Opportunities should be especially strong in the financial services, communications, and utilities industries.

For customer service representatives with specific knowledge of a product or business, the outlook is very good, as quick, efficient customer service is valuable in any business. Additional training and education and proficiency in a foreign language will also make finding a job as a customer service representative an easier task.

FOR MORE INFORMATION

For information on customer service and other support positions, contact
Association of Support Professionals
122 Barnard Avenue
Watertown, MA 02472-3414
Tel: 617-924-3944
http://www.asponline.com

For information on jobs, training, workshops, and salaries, contact
Customer Care Institute
17 Dean Overlook NW
Atlanta, GA 30318-1663
Tel: 404-352-9291
Email: info@customercare.com
http://www.customercare.com

For information about the customer service industry, contact
HDI
102 South Tejon, Suite 1200
Colorado Springs, CO 80903-2242
Tel: 800-248-5667
Email: support@thinkhdi.com
http://www.thinkhdi.com

For information on international customer service careers and certification, contact
International Customer Service Association
24 Wernik Place
Metuchen, NJ 08840-2468
Tel: 732-767-0330
Email: info@icsatoday.org
http://www.icsatoday.org

Event Planners

OVERVIEW

The duties of *event planners* are varied, and may include establishing a site for an event; making travel, hotel, and food arrangements; and planning the program and overseeing the registration. The planner may be responsible for negotiating, planning, and coordinating a major worldwide convention, or the planner may be involved with a small, in-house meeting involving only a few people. Some professional associations, government agencies, nonprofit organizations, political groups, and educational institutions hire event planners or have employees on staff who have these responsibilities. Many of these organizations and companies outsource their event planning responsibilities to firms that specialize in these services, such as marketing, public relations, and event planning firms. In addition, many event and meeting planners are independent consultants.

Some event planners' services are also used on a personal level to plan class or family reunions, birthday parties, weddings, or anniversaries. There are approximately 51,000 event planners employed in the United States.

HISTORY

According to the *National Directory of Occupational Titles and Codes*, the meeting management profession was recognized as a career in the early 1990s. As corporations have specialized and expanded their companies to include facilities and employees worldwide, the logistics of company meetings and events have become more complex. Planning a meeting that brings together employees and directors from around the world requires advanced

School Subjects
Business
English
Foreign language

Personal Skills
Communication/ideas
Leadership/management

Work Environment
Primarily indoors
One location with some travel

Minimum Education Level
Bachelor's degree

Salary Range
$26,880 to $43,530 to $74,740+

Certification or Licensing
Voluntary

Outlook
Faster than the average

DOT
169

GOE
11.01.01

NOC
1226

O*NET-SOC
13-1121.00

planning to acquire a site, make travel and hotel arrangements, book speakers and entertainment, and arrange for catering.

Similarly, the growth of the convention and trade show industry has resulted in the need for persons with skills specific to the planning, marketing, and execution of a successful show. Conventions, trade shows, meetings, and corporate travel have become a big business in recent years, accounting for more than $80 billion in annual spending.

The scope of meetings has changed as well. Technological advances now allow meetings to be conducted via the Internet, through video-conferencing or closed circuit television, or by setting up conference calls.

THE JOB

Event planners have a variety of duties depending on their specific title and the firm they work for or the firms they work with. Generally, planners organize and plan an event such as a meeting, a special open house, a convention, or a specific celebration.

Meetings might consist of a small interdepartmental meeting, a board meeting, an all-employee meeting, an in-house training session, a stockholders' meeting, or a meeting with vendors or distributors. When arranging these events, meeting planners usually check the calendars of key executives to establish a meeting time that fits into their schedules. Planners reserve meeting rooms, training rooms, or outside facilities for the event. They visit outside sites to make sure they are appropriate for that specific event. Planners notify people of the time, place, and date of the event and set up registration procedures, if necessary. They arrange for food, room layout, audiovisual equipment, instructors, computers, sound equipment, and telephone equipment as required.

In some cases, a company may employ an in-house meeting planner who is responsible for small- to medium-sized events. When a large meeting, trade show, conference, open house, or convention is planned, the in-house event planner may contract with outside meeting planners to assist with specific responsibilities such as registration, catering, and display setup. Some companies have their own trade show or convention managers on staff.

Convention, trade show, or *conference managers* negotiate and communicate with other enterprises related to the convention or trade show industry such as hotel and catering sales staff, speaker's bureaus, and trade staff such as *electricians* or *laborers* who set up convention display areas. They may also be responsible for contracting the transportation of the equipment and supplies to and from the event site. The manager usually works with an established budget and negotiates fees with these enterprises and enters contracts with them. Additional contracts may also need to be negotiated with professionals to handle registration, marketing, and public relations for the event.

Managers and planners need to be aware of legal aspects of trade show set-ups such as fire code regulations, floor plans, and space limitations, and make sure they are within these guidelines. They often need to get these arrangements approved in writing. Good record keeping and communication skills are used daily. The convention manager may have staff to handle the sales, registration, marketing, logistics, or other specific aspects of the event, or these duties may be subcontracted to another firm.

Some convention planners are employed specifically by convention and visitors' bureaus, the tourism industry, or by exhibit halls or convention facilities. Their job responsibilities may be specific to one aspect of the show, or they may be required to do any or all of the abovementioned duties. Some convention and trade show managers may work for the exposition center or association and be responsible for selling booth space at large events.

Special event coordinators are usually employed by large corporations who hold numerous special events or by firms who contract their special event planning services to companies, associations, or religious, political, or educational groups. A special event coordinator

Event planners participate in a strategy session before a conference. *(Jeff Greenberg/The Image Works)*

is responsible for planning, organizing, and implementing a special event such as an open house, an anniversary, the dedication of a new facility, a special promotion or sale, an ordination, a political rally, or a victory celebration. This coordinator works with the company or organization and determines the purpose of the special event, the type of celebration desired, the site, the budget, the attendees, the food and entertainment preferences, and the anticipated outcome. The special event planner then coordinates the vendors and equipment necessary to successfully hold this event. The coordinator works closely with the client at all times to ensure that the event is being planned as expected. Follow-up assessment of the event is usually part of the services offered by the special event coordinator.

Party planners are often employed by individuals, families, or small companies to help them plan a party for a special occasion. Many party planners are independent contractors who work out of their homes or are employees of small firms. Party planners may help plan weddings, birthdays, christenings, bar or bat mitzvahs, anniversaries, or other events. They may be responsible for the entire event including the invitations, catering, decorating, entertainment, serving, and cleanup, or planners may simply perform one or two aspects such as contracting with a magician for a children's birthday party, recommending a menu, or greeting and serving guests.

REQUIREMENTS

High School
If you are interested in entering the field of event planning, you should take high school classes in business, English, and speech. Because many conferences and meetings are international in scope, you may also want to take foreign language and geography courses. In addition, computer science classes will be beneficial.

Postsecondary Training
Almost all coordinators and planners must have a four-year college degree to work for a company, corporation, convention, or travel center. Some institutions offer bachelor's degrees in meeting planning; however, degrees in business, English, communications, marketing, public relations, sales, or travel would also be a good fit for a career as a meetings manager, convention planner, or special event coordinator. Many directors and planners who become company heads have earned graduate degrees.

Some small firms, convention centers, or exhibit facilities may accept persons with associate's degrees or travel industry certification for certain planning positions. Party planners may not always need education beyond high school, but advancement opportunities will be more plentiful with additional education.

Certification or Licensing

There are some professional associations for planners that offer certification programs. For example, Meeting Professionals International offers the certification in meeting management designation. The International Association of Exhibitions and Events offers the certified in exhibition management designation. The Convention Industry Council offers the certified meeting professional designation. The Society of Government Meeting Professionals offers the certified government meeting professional designation. See For More Information at the end of this article for contact information.

Other Requirements

To be an event planner, you must have excellent organizational skills, the ability to plan projects and events, and the ability to think creatively. You must be able to work well with people and anticipate their needs in advance. You should be willing to pitch in to get a job done even though it may not be part of your duties. In a situation where there is an unforeseen crisis, you need to react quickly and professionally. Planners should have good negotiating and communication skills and be assertive but tactful.

EXPLORING

High school guidance counselors can supply information on event planners or convention coordinators. Public and school librarians may also be able to provide useful books, magazines, and pamphlets. Searching the Internet for companies that provide event-planning services can give you an idea of the types of services that they offer. Professional associations related to the travel, convention, and meeting industries may have career information available to students. Some of these organizations are listed at the end of this article.

Attending local trade shows and conventions will provide insight into the operations of this industry. Also, some exhibit and convention halls may hire students to assist with various aspects of trade show operations. You can learn more about this profession by subscribing to magazines such as *Meetings & Conventions* (http://www.mcmag.com/).

Some party planners may hire assistants to help with children's birthday parties or other special events; contact party planners in your area to see if you could work for them. You might also try your hand at party planning. Organize and plan a large family event, such as a birthday, anniversary, graduation, or retirement celebration. You will have to find a location, hire caterers or assign family members to bring specific food items, send invitations, purchase and arrange decorations, and organize entertainment, all according to what your budget allows.

You can also gain business experience through school activities. Join the business club, run for student council, or head up the prom committee to learn how to plan and carry out events.

EMPLOYERS

Approximately 51,000 event planners are employed in the United States. Many large corporations or institutions worldwide hire meeting managers, convention managers, or event planners to handle their specific activities. Although some companies may not have employees with the specific title of event planner or meeting manager, these skills are very marketable and these duties may be part of another job title. In many companies, these duties may be part of a position within the marketing, public relations, or corporate communications department.

Convention facilities, exhibit halls, training and educational institutions, travel companies, and health care facilities also hire event planners. Hotels often hire planners to handle meetings and events held within their facilities. Large associations usually maintain an event planning staff for one or more annual conventions or business meetings for their members.

Job opportunities are also available with companies that contract out event and meeting planning services. Many of these companies have positions that specialize in certain aspects of the planning service, such as travel coordinator, exhibit planner, or facilities negotiator, or they have people who perform specific functions such as trade show display setup, registration, and follow-up reporting. Planners interested in jobs with the convention and trade show industries or hotels may find that larger cities have more demand for planners and offer higher salaries.

Experienced meeting planners or convention managers may choose to establish their own businesses or independently contract out their services. Party planning may also be a good independent business venture.

STARTING OUT

An internship at a visitors and convention bureau, exhibit center, or with a travel agency or meeting planning company is a good way to meet and network with other people in this field. Attending trade shows might offer a chance to speak with people about the field and to discuss any contacts they might have.

Some colleges and universities may offer job placement for people seeking careers in meeting planning or in the convention and trade show industries. Professional associations related to these industries are also good contacts for someone starting out. Classified ads and trade magazines may also offer some job leads.

ADVANCEMENT

Advancement opportunities for people in the event planning field are good. Experienced planners can expect to move into positions of increased responsibility. They may become senior managers and executive directors of private businesses, hotels, convention facilities, exhibit halls, travel corporations, museums, or other facilities. They can advance within a corporation to a position with more responsibilities or they may go into the planning business for themselves. Planners who have established a good reputation in the industry are often recruited by other firms or facilities and can advance their careers with these opportunities.

EARNINGS

According to the U.S. Department of Labor, meeting and convention planners earned a median annual salary of $43,530 in 2007. The lowest paid 10 percent earned less than $26,880, and the highest paid 10 percent earned more than $74,740.

Benefits may vary depending on the position and the employer but generally include vacation, sick leave, insurance, and other work-related benefits.

WORK ENVIRONMENT

Work environments vary with the planner's title and job responsibilities, but generally planners can expect to work in a business setting as part of a team. Prior to the opening of a convention or trade show, the planner's initial planning work will usually be done in a clean environment with modern equipment. Working in convention and trade show environments, however, can be noisy, crowded, and distracting. In addition, the days can be long and may require standing for hours.

If the planner is involved with supervising the setup or dismantling of a trade show or convention, the work can be dirty and physically demanding. Although most facilities have crews that assist with setup, meeting planners occasionally get involved with last-minute changes and may need to do some physical lifting of equipment, tables, or chairs.

Event planners can usually expect to work erratic hours, often putting in long days prior to the event and the day the event is actually held. Travel is often part of the job requirements and may include working and/or traveling nights and on the weekends.

OUTLOOK

Job opportunities for event planners will continue to grow faster than the average through 2016, according to the U.S. Department of Labor. The introduction of new technology enables more meetings to take place than ever before. Conventions, trade shows, meetings, and incentive travel support more than 1.5 million American jobs, according to the Professional Convention Management Association. These events account for more than $80 billion in spending annually. Opportunities should be best for event planners employed by medical and pharmaceutical associations.

FOR MORE INFORMATION

For information on certification and event planning, contact
Convention Industry Council
700 North Fairfax Street, Suite 510
Alexandria, VA 22314-2090
Tel: 571-527-3116
http://www.conventionindustry.org

For information on certification, contact
International Association of Exhibitions and Events
12700 Park Central Drive, Suite 308
Dallas, TX 75251-1313
Tel: 972-458-8002
http://www.iaee.com

For information on postsecondary training programs, scholarships, and certification, contact
Meeting Professionals International
3030 Lyndon B. Johnson Freeway, Suite 1700
Dallas, TX 75234-2759
Tel: 972-702-3000

Email: feedback@mpiweb.org
http://www.mpiweb.org

For information on career development, contact
Professional Convention Management Association
2301 South Lake Shore Drive, Suite 1001
Chicago, IL 60616-1419
Tel: 877-827-7262
Email: administration@pcma.org
http://www.pcma.org

For information on certification, contact
Society of Government Meeting Professionals
908 King Street, Lower Level
Alexandria, VA 22314-3047
Tel: 703-549-0892
http://www.sgmp.org

For information on careers in the field of event planning, contact
Society of Independent Show Organizers
2601 Ocean Park Boulevard, Suite 200
Santa Monica, CA 90405-5250
Tel: 877-YES-SISO
E-mail: info@siso.org
http://www.siso.org

INTERVIEW

Michael Walsh is the president of Walsh Productions. He has worked in the field for more than 28 years. Michael discussed his career with the editors of Careers in Focus: Business.

Q. What are your primary and secondary job duties?

A. My primary job duty is to technically direct and manage corporate business meetings. My secondary responsibility would be handling anything and everything else that might occur at the event.

Q. What do you like most about your job?

A. The thing I like the most is the project basis of my job. I have a start date for a project and know exactly when the project will end. I enjoy the sense of accomplishment when the meeting ends successfully.

Q. What advice would you give to high school students who are interested in this career?

A. I would recommend that anyone interested in business communication be as technologically diversified as possible. Take advantage of any computer courses, including graphic arts and CAD design. Observe and learn from whomever you can and do not be afraid to ask questions. Get involved in theater, audiovisual clubs, and any organizations where you can help to produce events.

Q. What are the most important professional qualities for event planners?

A. The most important professional quality that one must possess is to have a positive, can-do attitude. Having a proficient knowledge of your customer is essential, but no one wants to be associated with a negative or disagreeable person.

Q. What is the employment outlook for your field?

A. The employment outlook in my field looks as good as ever. I am a firm believer that if you provide a service that is above and beyond others in your field, you will stand out and always succeed.

Executive Recruiters

OVERVIEW

Executive recruiters are hired by businesses to locate, research, and interview candidates for hard-to-fill employment positions, mainly on the junior-to-senior management levels. Such recruiters work for executive search firms and are paid by clients either on a commission basis or flat fee. There are approximately 10,000 executive recruiters employed by search firms located throughout the United States.

HISTORY

Although most companies have competent in-house human resource departments, filling a top management position is often a lengthy and difficult process. Many times, human resource departments are not able to reach or identify the most qualified candidates. Also, a measure of privacy is lost if an entire department is aware of the need for a replacement. Companies are increasingly turning to a third party—the executive recruiter—for their employment needs.

Executive search firms fall into one of two categories: retained or contingency. *Retainer recruiters* work with upper-level management positions, such as CEOs or CFOs, with salary expectations averaging $150,000 or higher. They are exclusively contracted by a company or other entity to bring new executives on board. Retainer recruiters work on a flat-fee basis, or more commonly, for a percentage of the candidate's first-year salary and bonus. Commission percentages can range anywhere from 10 to 35 percent, although the industry standard is about a third of the candidate's proposed salary package. Executive recruiters, because of the high-level management

QUICK FACTS

School Subjects
Business
Psychology
Speech

Personal Skills
Communication/ideas
Leadership/management

Work Environment
Primarily indoors
Primarily multiple locations

Minimum Education Level
Bachelor's degree

Salary Range
$50,000 to $175,000 to
$250,000+

Certification or Licensing
Voluntary

Outlook
Faster than the average

DOT
166

GOE
13.01.01

NOC
N/A

O*NET-SOC
13-1071.02

positions they are assigned to fill and the exclusivity of their contract, usually take longer to complete their task—anywhere from three to six months, or more. The more qualities the company is looking for in a candidate, the longer the search.

The *contingency recruiter* deals with junior- to mid-level executive positions paying $50,000 to $150,000. Such recruiters are paid only if the candidate they present is hired for the job; pay is usually a percentage of the first-year salary package. Many times, however, a company will have more than one contingency firm working to fill a single position. Because of this, contingency recruiters are not guaranteed a fee and they may spend less time on their search. Some contingency recruiters also charge on an hourly basis or may work for a flat fee.

THE JOB

Most companies—from Fortune 500 firms to colleges and universities to small businesses—at one time or another have come across the need to replace an important executive or administrator. Because of restraints such as time, privacy, or resources, many businesses opt to use the services of an executive recruiter. The task begins once the search firm is retained (notified of the job opening) and is asked to find the best possible candidate.

The recruiter first evaluates the needs and structure of the company and the specifications of the open position. Then a written draft of the job description is made, detailing the title, job definition, responsibilities, and compensation. At this time, a wish list is composed of every possible quality, talent, skill, and educational background the perfect job candidate should possess. It is up to the recruiter to match these specifications as closely as possible.

Once a written contract is approved by the client, then the real work begins. The three traditional job functions in the recruitment industry are: researcher, associate, and consultant. Researchers conduct research to find possible candidates. They look through directories and databases, and network with contacts familiar with the field. They read trade papers and magazines as well as national newspapers such as the *Wall Street Journal* and the *New York Times*. Business sections of newspapers often include write-ups of industry leaders. Recruiters also receive résumés from people looking to change employment, which they may use for future reference. It's imperative recruiters stay current with the field they specialize in; they need to be familiar with the key players as well as important technological advances that may change the scope of the industry.

Once a long list is assembled, associates contact the prospective candidates, usually by telephone. Candidates who are interested and qualified are screened further; references are checked fully. Consultants conduct personal interviews with promising candidates who make the short list of hopefuls. Consultants also manage client relationships and develop new business for the firm.

The goal of retainer executive recruiters is to present three to five of the best candidates to a client for final interviews. Contingency recruiters, on the other hand, will present many qualified candidates to the client, to better their chance of filling the position. Executive recruiters will not edit resumes or coach on the interview process, but some will offer information on where candidates stand after the initial interview and give advice on strengths and perceived weaknesses.

A search for the perfect executive is a lengthy process. Most searches take anywhere from one month to a year or more. Once the position is filled, recruiters conduct one or more follow ups to make sure the employee's transition into the company is smooth. Any conflicts or discrepancies are addressed and often mediated by, or along with, the search firm. Some executive search firms offer some kind of guarantee with their work. If the hired employee leaves a firm within a specified period of time or does not work out as anticipated, then the recruiter will find a replacement for a reduced fee or at no charge.

REQUIREMENTS

High School

To prepare for a career as an executive recruiter, you should take business, speech, English, and mathematics classes in high school. Psychology and sociology courses will teach you how to recognize personality characteristics that may be key in helping you determine which job candidates would best fit a position.

Postsecondary Training

You will need at least a bachelor's degree and several years of work experience to become an executive recruiter. Postsecondary courses helpful to this career include communications, marketing, and business administration. Some colleges offer undergraduate degrees in human resources management or business degrees with a concentration in human resources management. To have more job opportunities, you may also consider getting a master's degree in one of these fields. Most recruiters move into this industry after successful

Read More About It

Cawley, Charrissa D. *The Complete Guide to Owning and Operating a Home-Based Recruiting Business: A Step-By-Step Business Plan for Entrepreneurs.* Lincoln, Nebr.: Writers Club Press, 2001.

Entrepreneur Press. *Start Your Own Executive Recruiting Business.* 2d ed. Newburgh, N.Y.: Entrepreneur Press, 2007.

Foster, Michael. *Recruiting on the Web: Smart Strategies for Finding the Perfect Candidate.* New York: McGraw-Hill, 2002.

Kennedy Information. *The Directory of Executive Recruiters, 2009–2010.* Peterborough, N.H.: Kennedy Information, 2006.

careers in their particular areas of expertise (for example, health care, finance, publishing, or computers) and they come to the field with a variety of educational backgrounds.

Certification or Licensing

The Association of Executive Search Consultants (AESC) offers the certified researcher/associate designation to workers in the field. Contact the association for certification requirements.

Other Requirements

Executive recruiters need strong people skills. Good communicators are in demand, especially those who can maintain a high level of integrity and confidentiality. Recruiters are privy to sensitive company and employee information that could prove disastrous if leaked to the public.

The most powerful tool in this industry is a network of good contacts. Since executive recruiters come on board after working in the field for which they are now recruiting, they are usually familiar with who's who in the business.

EXPLORING

Familiarize yourself with business practices by joining or starting a business club at your school. Being a part of a speech or debate team is a great way to develop excellent speaking skills, which are necessary in this field. Hold mock interviews with family or friends, and get work and volunteer experience in your specialized field (for example, health care or publishing). Professional associations, such as The International Association for Corporate and Professional Recruiters, are also good sources of information. Visit this association's Web site (http://www.iacpr.org) to learn more.

EMPLOYERS

Executive search firms of all sizes are located throughout the United States. Most specialize in placement in a particular field, for example, chemical engineering or advertising. For a list of search firms, you may want to refer to the *Directory of Executive Recruiters*, also known in the industry as the "Red Book." Search firms in the United States employ approximately 10,000 executive recruiters, according to an estimate by *Executive Recruiter News*.

STARTING OUT

A common starting point in this industry is a position at a contingency search firm, or even at an outplacement center. Responsibilities may be limited at first, but a successful and consistent track record should lead to bigger clients, more placements, and higher commissions. Many executive recruiters were recruited into the field themselves, especially if they were well known in their industry. It is important to market yourself and your accomplishments while you work in entry-level positions. Circulate among the movers and shakers of your company, as well as those of the competition. They may prove to be valuable contacts for the future. Most importantly, cultivate relationships with any recruitment firms that may call; you'll never know when their assistance may be desired, or necessary.

ADVANCEMENT

A typical advancement path in this industry would be a transfer to a retainer-based search firm. Retained search firms deal with the upper-echelon administrative positions that pay top salaries, translating to higher commissions for the recruiter.

Let's say you've already paid your dues and worked successfully at a retainer search firm. What next? You may want to negotiate for partnership or opt to call the shots and start a firm of your own.

EARNINGS

Executive recruiters are paid well for their efforts. Contingency recruiters, who get paid only if their candidate is hired, typically charge a fee from 25 percent to 35 percent of the candidate's first-year cash compensation.

Retained recruiters average fees of one-third of the candidate's first-year cash compensation. The employer also usually pays any expenses incurred by the recruiter. According to *U.S. News & World Report*, average entry-level positions pay from $50,000 to $100,000 annually, while mid-level recruiters earn from $100,000 to $250,000. Top earners, those working for larger retainer recruiting firms, can make more than $250,000 a year. The U.S. Department of Labor reports that executive recruiters earned salaries that ranged from less than $50,683 to $100,686 or more in 2008.

Along with their salary, all recruiters are offered a benefits package that includes health insurance, paid vacations, and sick time or paid disability.

WORK ENVIRONMENT

Many recruiters work 50 to 70 hours a week; it's not uncommon for recruiters to spend several days a week on the road meeting clients, interviewing, or doing candidate research. Also, aspiring recruiters should expect to spend most of their day on the phone.

OUTLOOK

The executive search industry should have a good future. Potential clients include not only large international corporations but also universities, the government, and smaller businesses. Smaller operations are aware that having a solid executive or administrator may make the difference between turning a profit and not being in business at all. Many times, search firm services are used to conduct industry research or to scope out the competition. Executive search firms now specialize in many fields of employment—health care, engineering, or accounting, for example.

The era of company loyalty and employment for life is over in the corporate world. Many savvy workers campaign aggressively and will transfer if offered a larger salary, improved benefits, and stock options—in short, a better employment future. Employers, on the other hand, realize the importance in having qualified and experienced employees at the helm of their business. Most companies are willing to pay the price, whether a retainer fee or commission, to find just the right person for the job.

According to the Association of Executive Search Consultants (AESC), it is becoming more important for executive recruiters to operate on a global basis. They must be able to conduct searches for clients and candidates in other countries. Peter Felix, president of AESC, says, "Today, the retained executive search business is a $10 billion industry operating in all the major economies of the world. In this era of the knowledge society where executive talent is so important, executive search is seen increasingly as a critical management tool."

FOR MORE INFORMATION

For information on certification, contact
Association of Executive Search Consultants
12 East 41st Street, 17th Floor
New York, NY 10017-6276
Tel: 212-398-9556
Email: aesc@aesc.org
http://www.aesc.org

For industry information, contact
International Association for Corporate & Professional Recruitment
327 North Palm Drive, Suite 201
Beverly Hills, CA 90210-4167
Tel: 310-550-0304
Email: office@iacpr.org
http://www.iacpr.org

National Association of Executive Recruiters
Tel: 847-885-1453
Email: naerinfo@naer.org
http://www.naer.org

For a copy of the industry newsletter Executive Recruiter News *or the* Directory of Executive Recruiters, *contact*
Kennedy Information
One Phoenix Mill Lane, 3rd Floor
Peterborough, NH 03458-1467
Tel: 800-531-0007
Email: bookstore@kennedyinfo.com
http://www.kennedyinfo.com

Franchise Owners

School Subjects
Business
Mathematics

Personal Skills
Following instructions
Leadership/management

Work Environment
Primarily indoors
Primarily one location

Minimum Education Level
Some postsecondary training

Salary Range
$0 to $30,000 to $100,000+

Certification or Licensing
Required by certain
    franchisers (certification)
Required by certain states
    (licensing)

Outlook
About as fast as the average

DOT
N/A

GOE
N/A

NOC
N/A

O*NET-SOC
N/A

OVERVIEW

A *franchise owner* contracts with a company to sell that company's products or services. After paying an initial fee and agreeing to pay the company a certain percentage of revenue, the franchise owner can use the company's name, logo, and guidance. McDonald's, Subway, and KFC are some of the top franchised companies that have locations all across the country. Franchises, however, are not limited to the fast food industry. Today, franchises are available in a wide variety of business areas including computer service, lawn care, real estate, and even hair salons. According to a survey by PricewaterhouseCoopers, the franchising sector creates 18 million jobs in the United States and yields $1.53 trillion in economic output annually.

HISTORY

Know anybody with an antique Singer sewing machine? Chances are, it was originally sold by one of the first franchise operations. During the Civil War, the Singer Sewing Machine Company recognized the cost-efficiency of franchising and allowed dealers across the country to sell its sewing machines. Coca-Cola, as well as the Ford Motor Company and other automobile manufacturers, followed Singer's lead in the early 20th century by granting individuals the rights to sell their products. Franchising, however, didn't fully catch on until after World War II, when the needs for products and services across the country grew to keep up with the population boom. Ray Kroc jumped on the bandwagon with his McDonald's restaurants in the 1950s. Since then, the McDonald's

franchise has become one of the top moneymaking franchise opportunities of all time.

Franchises have changed somewhat over the last 20 to 30 years.
Abuses of the franchise system brought new government regulations in the 1970s, and the government has been actively involved
in protecting the rights of both franchisers and franchisees. Also,
single-unit ownership, the "mom and pop" operations, is giving way
to multiple-unit ownership; a majority of franchisees now own more
than one of the franchiser's units.

THE JOB

Today, industry experts report that franchises are responsible for
nearly 50 percent of all retail sales in the United States, and this
figure is expected to grow through the 21st century. *Franchisers*
(those companies that sell franchise businesses) and *franchisees*
(those who buy the businesses) are sharing in the more than $1.5
trillion a year that franchise businesses take in. While everyone
probably has a favorite business or two—maybe the neighborhood
Krispy Kreme with its fresh crullers or the 7-11 down the street
with its gallon-sized sodas—not everyone may realize that these

Franchise owner Gig Wilkowsky poses with signs that his company,
Signs By Tomorrow, creates. Franchise owners need self-motivation
and discipline in order to make their franchise unit successful.
(AP Photo/Gregory Smith)

are franchised establishments. For those interested in starting their own businesses, becoming franchisees may offer just the right mix of risk and security. Any new business venture comes with a certain amount of risk, but franchises offer the new owners the security of a name and product that customers are used to and are willing to seek out. Someone with money to invest, the willingness to work hard and sometimes long hours, and the desire to operate a retail business may be able to become the successful franchisee, sharing in the franchiser's success.

There's a franchise for practically every type of product and service imaginable. In addition to the familiar McDonald's and Burger King, other franchise operations exist: businesses that offer temporary employment services, maid services, weight control centers, and custom picture framing, to name a few. In fact, the International Franchise Association (IFA) reports that there are approximately 75 different industries that make use of the franchise system. No matter what business a person is interested in, there are probably franchise opportunities available.

Depending on the size and nature of the franchise, owners' responsibilities will differ. Those who are able to make a large initial investment may also be able to hire managers and staff members to assist them. Those running a smaller business will need to handle most, if not all, of the job responsibilities themselves. Although there should be assistance from the franchiser in terms of training, marketing guidance, and established business systems, the business is essentially the franchisee's own. The franchisee has paid an initial franchise fee, purchased equipment, rented business space, and agreed to make royalty payments to the franchiser. Any franchisee must handle administrative details, such as record keeping, creating budgets, and preparing reports for the franchiser. A franchisee is also responsible for hiring (and firing) employees, scheduling work hours, preparing payroll, and keeping track of inventory. Using the franchiser's marketing methods, the franchisee advertises the business. The practices and systems of franchisers differ, so those interested in this work need to carefully research the franchise before buying into it.

Some owners work directly with the clientele. Of course, someone who owns multiple units of the McDonald's franchise probably won't be taking orders at the counter; but someone who owns a single unit of a smaller operation, like a pool maintenance service, may be actively involved in the work at hand, in dealing with the customers, and in finding new customers.

Donna Weber of Redmond, Washington, owns a Jazzercise franchise. Jazzercise is the world's largest dance fitness franchise corporation, with 7,500 instructors leading more than 32,000 classes weekly in 32 countries. "I own and teach seven Jazzercise classes a week in two suburbs around the Seattle area," Weber says. After investing with an initial low franchise fee, Weber went through considerable training and testing; the training involves instruction on exercise physiology, dance/exercise technique, and safety issues, as well as instruction on the business aspects of owning a franchise. After training, Weber received certification and started her business. She pays a monthly fee to Jazzercise and in return receives choreography notes to new songs and videos demonstrating the exercises.

In addition to conducting classes, Weber spends some part of every workday preparing paperwork for the corporate headquarters. "I keep track of my students' attendance and write personal postcards to those I haven't seen in a while, those who are having birthdays, those who need some personal recognition for a job well done, etc.," says Weber, who must also regularly learn new routines. "I teach three different formats," she says, "regular aerobics, step, and a circuit-training class each week, so there is a lot of prep to do a good, safe class."

The franchisee's experience will be affected by the name recognition of the business. If it's a fairly new business, the franchisee may have to take on much of the responsibility of promoting it. If it is a well-established business, customers and clients already know what to expect from the operation.

REQUIREMENTS

High School
Business, math, economics, and accounting courses will be the most valuable to you in preparing for franchise ownership. Before buying into a franchise, you'll have to do a lot of research into the company, analyzing local demographics to determine whether a business is a sound investment. English classes will help you develop the research skills you'll need. In addition, you will need to hone your communication skills, which will be essential in establishing relationships with franchisers and customers. Take computer classes since it is virtually impossible to work in today's business world without knowing how to use a computer or the Internet. If you already know of a particular area that interests you—such as food service, fashion, or, like Donna Weber, fitness—take classes that will help you learn more about it. Such classes may include home economics, art, dance, or physical education.

Postsecondary Training

Because there is such a variety of franchise opportunities available, there is no single educational path for everyone to take on the road to owning a franchise. Keep in mind, however, that when franchisers review your application for the right to purchase a unit, they'll take into consideration your previous experience in the area. Obviously, a real estate company is unlikely to take a risk on you if you've never had any experience as a broker. In addition, there are some franchise opportunities that require degrees; for example, to own an environmental consulting agency, a business that helps companies meet government environmental standards, you'll have to be an engineer or geologist (careers that, in most cases, require at least a bachelor's degree). However, there are also many companies willing to sell to someone wanting to break into a new business. Franchisers will often include special training as part of the initial franchise fee.

Experts in the field stress the importance of gaining work experience before starting out with your own business. Hone your sales, management, and people skills and take the time to learn about the industry that interests you. Even if you don't plan on getting a college degree, consider taking some college-level courses in subjects such as business and finance. One recent survey of franchisees found that more than 80 percent had attended college or had a college degree. This reflects the fact that many franchisees have worked for many years in other professions in order to have the money and security needed for starting new businesses. Some organizations and schools, for example, the Schulze School of Entrepreneurship at the University of St. Thomas (http://www.stthomas.edu/business/schulze school/default.html), offer courses for prospective franchisees.

Certification or Licensing

Some franchisers have their own certification process and require their franchisees to go through training. You may also want to receive the certified franchise executive designation offered by the Institute for Certified Franchise Executives, an organization affiliated with the IFA. This certification involves completing a certain number of courses in topics such as economics and franchise law, participating in events such as seminars or conventions, and work experience. Although certification is voluntary, it will show your level of education and commitment to the field as well as give you the opportunity to network with other franchise professionals.

You may also need to obtain a small business license to own a franchise unit in your state. Regulations vary depending on the state and the type of business, so it is important that you check with your state's licensing board for specifics before you invest in a franchise.

Other Requirements

As with any small business, you need self-motivation and discipline in order to make your franchise unit successful. Although you'll have some help from your franchiser, the responsibilities of ownership are your own. You'll also need a good credit rating to be eligible for a bank loan, or you'll need enough money of your own for the initial investment. You should be fairly cautious—every year many people are taken in by fraudulent franchise schemes. At the same time, however, you should feel comfortable taking some risks.

EXPLORING

One relatively easy way to learn about franchising is to do some research on the Web. The International Franchise Association, for example, hosts a very informative Web site (http://www.franchise.org). The association also offers the magazine *Franchising World*. Also, check out your public library or bookstores for the many business magazines that report on small business opportunities. Many of these magazines, such as *Entrepreneur* (http://www.entrepreneur.com), publish special editions that deal specifically with franchises.

Join your high school's business club, a group that may give you the opportunity to meet business leaders in your community. Find a local franchise owner and ask to meet with him or her for an information interview. Discuss the pros and cons of franchise ownership, find out about the owner's educational and professional background, and ask him or her for general advice. Also, most franchise companies will send you brochures about their franchise opportunities. Request some information and read about what's involved in owning a franchise unit.

Facts About Franchises

- There are approximately 900,000 franchised establishments in the United States.
- The most popular types of franchises (by number of establishments) in 2005 were business services (25 percent), quick service restaurants (21.7 percent), retail products and services (10.2 percent), personal services (9.9 percent), food retail (7.9 percent), and table/full service restaurants (5.5 percent).
- Franchising has the "greatest impact on jobs and payrolls" in Arizona, Mississippi, Nevada, and New Mexico.

Source: International Franchise Association

Think about what industry interests you, such as services, fast food, computers, or health and fitness. Come up with your own ideas for a franchise business and do some research to find out if this business already exists. If it does, there may be a part-time or summer job opportunity there for you. If it doesn't, keep the idea in mind for your future but go ahead and get some work experience now. Many franchises hire high school students, and even if you end up working at a Subway when what you're really interested in is lawn care, you'll still be gaining valuable experience dealing with customers, handling sales, and working with others.

EMPLOYERS

There are a number of franchise directories available that list hundreds of franchise opportunities in diverse areas. While some franchisers sell units all across the country, others only do business in a few states. Some of the most successful franchises can guarantee a franchisee great revenue, but these franchise units can require hundreds of thousands of dollars in initial investment.

Many franchisees own more than one franchise unit with a company; some even tie two different franchises together in a practice called "cross-branding." For example, a franchisee may own a pizza franchise as well as an ice cream franchise housed in the same restaurant. Another combination owners find popular is having a convenience store that also houses a fast food outlet.

STARTING OUT

Before you invest a cent or sign any papers, you should do extensive research into the franchise, particularly if it's a fairly new company. There are many disreputable franchise operations, so you need to be certain of what you're investing in. Lawyers and franchise consultants offer their services to assist people in choosing franchises; some consultants also conduct seminars. The Federal Trade Commission publishes *A Consumer Guide to Buying a Franchise* and other relevant publications. The IFA also provides free franchise-buying advice.

You'll need money for the initial franchise fee and for the expenses of the first few years of business. You may pursue a loan from a bank, from business associates, or you may use your own savings. In some cases your start-up costs will be very low; in others you'll need money for a computer, rent, equipment, signs, and staff. According to the IFA, total start-up costs can range from less than $20,000 to more than $1,000,000, depending on the franchise selected and whether it is necessary to own or lease real estate to operate the business. Moreover, the initial franchise fee for most franchisers is between $10,000 and $30,000.

Some franchises can cost much less. Donna Weber's Jazzercise franchise required an initial $600 franchise fee. Although her business has been successful, she must share her gross income. "Twenty percent of that goes back to Jazzercise each month as a fee, I pay about 23 percent of the gross for monthly rent, and 8.6 percent to the state of Washington for sales tax collected on the price of my tickets. There are lots of women grossing $75,000 a year doing this, and there are some who choose to do this for fun and make nothing in return. It's all in how you make it work for you."

ADVANCEMENT

A new franchise unit usually takes a few years to turn profitable. Once the business has proved a success, franchisees may choose to invest in other franchise units with the same company. Franchise owners may also be able to afford to hire management and other staff to take on some of the many responsibilities of the business.

EARNINGS

The earnings for franchisees vary greatly depending on such factors as the type of franchise they own, the amount of money a franchisee was able to initially invest without taking a loan, the franchise's location, and the number of franchise units the franchisee owns. An International Franchise Association survey of 1,000 franchise owners found that the average yearly salary of this group was $91,630. Approximately 24 percent made more than $100,000 annually.

Since franchisees run their own businesses, they generally do not have paid sick days or holidays. In addition, they are typically responsible for providing their own insurance and retirement plans.

WORK ENVIRONMENT

Owning a franchise unit can be demanding, requiring work of 60 to 70 hours per week, but owners have the satisfaction of knowing that their business's success is a result of their own hard work. Some people look for franchise opportunities that are less demanding and may only require a part-time commitment. "I'm not getting rich," Donna Weber says, "but I love my job, and I love being my own boss. I can schedule my vacations when I want; we usually don't close our classes down, so we hire certified Jazzercise substitutes."

Franchise owners who handle all the business details themselves may consider this work to be very stressful. In addition, dealing with the hiring, management, and sometimes firing of staff can also be difficult. In some situations, much of a franchisee's work will be limited to an office setting; in other situations, such as with a home inspection service or a maid service, the franchisee drives to remote sites to work with clients. Some franchises are mobile in nature, and these will involve a lot of traveling within a designated region.

OUTLOOK

While some experts say that the success rate of franchises is very high and a great deal of money can be made with a franchise unit, others say franchising isn't as successful as starting an independent business. In every year since 1971, fewer than 5 percent of franchised outlets have failed, according to the U.S. Department of Commerce. However, when reporting figures, franchisers don't always consider a unit as failing if it is under different ownership, but still in operation. The employment outlook will depend on factors such as the economy—a downturn in the economy is always more difficult for new businesses—as well as the type of franchise. Overall, though, growth should be steady and about as fast as the average.

FOR MORE INFORMATION

For information about buying a franchise and a list of AAFD-accredited franchisers, contact
American Association of Franchisees & Dealers (AAFD)
PO Box 81887
San Diego, CA 92138-1887
Tel: 800-733-9858
Email: Benefits@aafd.org
http://www.aafd.org

Visit the FTC's Web site for information on franchising, including the publication A Consumer Guide to Buying a Franchise.
Federal Trade Commission (FTC)
600 Pennsylvania Avenue NW
Washington, DC 20580-0001
Tel: 202-326-2222
http://www.ftc.gov

For more information on franchising as well as a free newsletter, contact
FranchiseHelp
101 Executive Boulevard, 2nd Floor
Elmsford, NY 10523-1302
Tel: 800-401-1446
Email: company@franchisehelp.com
http://www.franchisehelp.com

For general information about franchising, specific franchise opportunities, and publications, contact
International Franchise Association
1501 K Street NW, Suite 350
Washington, DC 20005-1412
Tel: 202-628-8000
Email: ifa@franchise.org
http://www.franchise.org

Internet Executives

QUICK FACTS

School Subjects
Business
Computer science

Personal Skills
Communication/ideas
Leadership/management
Technical/scientific

Work Environment
Primarily indoors
One location with some
travel

Minimum Education Level
Bachelor's degree

Salary Range
$65,760 to $108,070 to
$173,109+

Certification or Licensing
Voluntary

Outlook
Faster than the average

DOT
N/A

GOE
09.01.01, 10.01.01, 13.01.01

NOC
0611

O*NET-SOC
11-1011.00, 11-1011.02,
11-1021.00, 11-3021.00,
11-3031.01

OVERVIEW

Internet executives plan, organize, manage, and coordinate the operations of businesses that engage in commerce over the Internet. These upper-level positions include presidents, chief operating officers, executive vice presidents, chief financial officers, chief information officers, chief technology officers, and regional and district managers. The majority of Internet executives are employed in large companies in urban areas.

HISTORY

Since the early 1990s, online business, often called e-commerce, has been extended to virtually every industry. Advertising, distance education programs, sales, banking, tax filing, Web conferencing, bill payment, and online auctions are just a few of the business outlets in which the Internet has profoundly played a role. Companies that have developed a Web presence in these industries, either in addition to or as a replacement for a brick-and-mortar-business, need management executives to run their online business dealings just as a traditional business needs a CEO. This is the job of Internet executives.

THE JOB

All businesses have specific goals and objectives that they strive to meet, such as making a certain profit or increasing the client base by a certain amount. Executives devise strategies and formulate policies to ensure that these objectives are met. In today's business world, many companies that first began as brick-and-mortar businesses now have a presence on the Internet. Additionally, many new companies, known as "dot-coms," are found only on the Internet. At both types of companies, Internet executives are the professionals who devise ways to meet their companies' objectives—making sales, providing services, or developing a customer base, for example—as they relate to the Internet.

Like executives in traditional companies, Internet executives have a wide range of titles and responsibilities. The positions include president, chairman, chief executive officer (who is sometimes the same person as the president or chairman), chief operating officer, chief financial officer, chief information officer, executive vice presidents, and the board of directors. *Presidents, chairmen,* and *chief executive officers (CEOs)* at companies with an Internet presence are leaders of the companies. They plan business objectives and develop policies to coordinate operations between divisions and departments and establish procedures for attaining objectives. They may review activity reports and financial statements to determine progress and revise operations as needed. They also direct and formulate funding for new and existing programs within their organizations.

Chief operating officers, or *COOs,* at dot-coms and other companies with an Internet presence are typically responsible for the day-to-day operations of the company. They may work to increase their companies' client base, improve sales, and develop operational and personnel policies. Depending on the type of business, other duties a COO may have include heading departments, such as marketing, engineering, or sales. Usually the COO directly reports to the top executive whether it is the CEO, chairman, or president. COOs typically have years of experience working in their industry and may also have worked at their particular company for years, moving up the corporate ranks while gaining knowledge about their companies' products and markets. Additionally, they have extensive knowledge of Internet capabilities and technologies available that will help their companies reach goals.

Some companies have an *executive vice president* who manages the activities of one or more departments, depending on the size of the organization. Executive vice presidents employed by very large organizations may be highly specialized; for example, they may oversee the activities of business managers of advertising, administrative services, data processing, property management, marketing, sales, purchasing, finance, human resources, industrial relations, transportation, or legal services. In smaller organizations, an executive vice president may supervise several of these departments.

Dot-coms and other companies with a presence on the Internet may also have a *chief financial officer,* who is responsible for managing the organization's financial issues, such as budgeting, capital expenditure planning, cash management activities, and various financial reviews and reports.

Chief information officers manage all aspects of their company's information technology and computer systems. They determine how these resources can best be used to meet company goals. This may include researching, purchasing, and overseeing set-up and use of technology systems, such as intranet, Internet, and computer networks. (For more information on this career, see the article Chief Information Officers.)

Management information systems directors oversee computer and information systems for an entire company. They often report to the chief information officer. They may manage an organization's employee help desk, recommend hardware and software upgrades, and ensure the security and availability of information technology services.

Chief technology officers evaluate and recommend new technologies that will help their organization reduce costs and increase revenue. They often report to the chief information officer.

All of these executive and management positions may be available at large companies, while the responsibilities of several of these positions may be combined into one role at smaller companies. Internet executives may work in any of these positions for companies that do business exclusively online or traditional businesses that also have an online presence. The common denominator among these executives is that they are all involved to some extent with figuring out how to use the Internet to enhance the capabilities and profitability of their businesses.

Rob Linxweiler, a consultant to a number of Internet companies in the Chicago area, says, "A downside of the industry is that sometimes it's hard to measure success on a daily or even weekly basis. We may accomplish two or three major projects per year, and those are the milestones by which we judge ourselves. It's possible to get mired in the day-to-day and fail to see the larger picture."

Linxweiler is quick to point out that there are many positives to an Internet executive's job, including working with interesting people. He also adds, "The work may not always be fascinating, but the technologies available can be used in some creative ways to overcome obstacles. I like to apply my creativity to problem solving."

Involvement in Internet commerce adds a new dimension for the consideration of executives. While most executives don't get directly involved in the day-to-day operation of the technology that drives their Internet business, an understanding of the technologies at work is crucial to the performance of their jobs. Executives will likely have to work directly with technology experts, so proficiency with the relevant technologies is a necessity. The combination of technological and business expertise Internet executives have makes these individuals among the most sought-after in the executive job market.

REQUIREMENTS

High School

If you are interested in a management career dealing with the Internet, you should plan on going to college after high school. Take a college preparatory curriculum, including classes in science, history, and government. Be sure to take as many computer science classes as possible so that you have a basic understanding of the technology that is available. Because an executive must communicate with a wide range of people, take as many English classes as possible to hone your communication skills. Speech classes are another way to improve these skills. Courses in mathematics and business are also excellent choices to help you prepare for this career. Learning a foreign language may also be helpful in preparing for today's global business market.

Postsecondary Training

Internet executives have diverse educational backgrounds. Many have a bachelor's degree in computer science, information management, information technology, information security, business administration, or a liberal arts field such as economics or communications. All Internet executives are expected to have experience with the information technology that applies to their field. While in college, you should keep up with your computer studies in addition to deciding what type of work interests you. Are you drawn to sales and marketing, for example, or does the actual manufacturing of a product interest you? A good way to find out is to get some hands-on experience through an internship or summer job. Your college career services office should be able to help you locate such a position with a business or organization that appeals to you.

Graduate and professional degrees are common among executives. Many executives in administrative, marketing, financial, and manufacturing activities have a master of business administration. Executives in highly technical manufacturing and research activities often have a master's degree or doctorate in a technical or scientific discipline.

Certification or Licensing

Voluntary computer- and Internet-related certifications are available from professional associations such as the Institute for Certification of Computing Professionals and the Institute of Certified Professional Managers. These designations are helpful in proving your abilities to an employer. The more certifications you have, the more you have to offer.

Other Requirements

An executive who manages other employees should have good communication and interpersonal skills. Rob Linxweiler advises, "Work on your communication skills. There is a surprising level of ambiguity in the technological arena, and the ability to say what you mean and be understood is crucial." He adds, "Hands-on experience with some technologies is also very important. The technologies change rapidly. It's not really relevant which particular system you have experience with, but an understanding of the basic processes and rules by which computer technologies operate is extremely important."

The ability to delegate work and think on your feet is often key to success in this career. Having strong organization skills is important since executives often have to juggle several tasks at the same time. Other important traits for Internet executives are intelligence, creativity, honesty, loyalty, decisiveness, intuition, and a sense of responsibility. Finally, successful executives should be interested in staying abreast of new developments in their industry and technology. They must constantly update their skills via seminars, college classes, and other learning methods.

EXPLORING

To explore your interest in the computer and technology aspect of this work, take every opportunity to work with computers. Surf the Web to visit sites of different businesses and organizations and find out what services they offer. Improve your computer skills by joining a users group, setting up your own Web page, and taking extra computer classes at a local community center or tech school.

You can gain management experience by participating in school clubs and school publications (such as the newspaper or yearbook). These activities will get you involved with planning, scheduling, managing other workers or volunteers, fund-raising, or budgeting.

Contact a local business executive—the best source would be one whose company also has a Web site—and ask for an information interview during which you can talk with him or her about this career. Some schools or community organizations arrange "job-shadowing," where interested young people can spend part of a day following selected employees to see what their job is like. Joining Junior Achievement (http://www.ja.org) is another good way to get involved with local businesses and learn about how they work.

Finally, get a part-time or summer job at a local business to get hands-on experience working in an office environment. Although your job may be that of cashier, you'll be able to see how the business is organized and run. You may also find a manager or executive there who can act as a mentor and give you advice.

EMPLOYERS

General managers and executives hold 2.1 million jobs in the United States, according to the U.S. Department of Labor. These jobs are found in every industry; however, more than 75 percent of these jobs are in the service industry—which is heavily involved in the Internet.

Businesses with an Internet presence are the norm in today's market. Almost all large retail businesses have some sort of presence on the World Wide Web, and their Web site is an essential part of their customer contact program for both sales and marketing. Besides working at large retail businesses, Internet executives may work in such areas as not-for-profit organizations, small start-up companies, and corporate consulting firms.

STARTING OUT

Executive positions are not entry-level jobs. Generally, those interested in becoming Internet executives start with a college degree and gain a significant amount of work experience. After you have decided what industry you are interested in, your college career services office should be able to help you locate your first job. Many companies also send representatives to college campuses to interview graduating students as potential hires. You may also want to attend recruitment and job fairs to find job openings. In addition, a past internship or summer work experience may provide you with contacts that lead to employment. You should research the field you are interested in to find out what might be the best point of entry.

After you have gained some work experience you may want to consider returning to school for a graduate degree. Or, you may be able to work your way up through your organization's management levels. Some organizations have executive management trainee programs available to their employees; other companies may pay for an employee's graduate schooling as long as the employee continues to work for the company. Many executives have a master of business administration, although higher degrees in computer science and related technology fields are becoming more common.

Once you have considerable training and management experience, you can move into an executive level position by directly applying to the corporate management. In addition, some executive search and placement firms specialize in job hunting for those involved with the Internet. *Digital agents,* specialists who work only with those seeking technology jobs, may also be a good source of employment leads.

Hiring standards for technology executives are still evolving, but it's clear that simply being well acquainted with the technologies is not enough. You will need significant experience in both business management and technology to meet the requirements of most of these positions.

ADVANCEMENT

Lower-level managers who demonstrate leadership, self-confidence, decisiveness, creativity, motivation, strong interpersonal skills, and flexibility are often considered for top executive positions. Rob Linxweiler says, "Good interpersonal skills are a must. Patience, enthusiasm, and the ability to listen to employees are indispensable skills that are often underrated. The ability to make good decisions and act on them is also vital. These are the building blocks of a strong leader, which is the most important thing an executive can be."

Advancement in smaller firms may come more slowly, while promotions may occur more quickly in larger firms. Managers can often improve their chances of advancement by participating in educational programs paid for by their employer. Managers who take company training programs broaden their knowledge of company policy and operations. Training programs sponsored by industry and trade associations and continuing education courses taken at colleges and universities can familiarize managers with the latest developments in management techniques. In recent years, large numbers of middle managers were laid off as companies streamlined operations. An employee's proven commitment to improving his or her knowledge of the business's field and computer information systems is important in establishing a reputation as a top professional. Regardless of the industry, the advancement path of executives at Internet companies is limited only by their interest, abilities, and willingness to work hard.

EARNINGS

Salary levels for Internet executives vary substantially, depending upon their level of responsibility, length of service, and the type, size, and location of the organization for which they work. Top executives in large firms can earn much more than executives in small firms. Also, executives employed in large metropolitan areas tend to earn higher salaries than workers in smaller cities—although this may be offset by the higher cost of living in large cities.

Computerworld reported the following average annual salaries (including bonuses) by specialty for Internet executives in 2008: chief information officers, $173,109; chief technology officers, $165,304; and directors of information technology, $120,649. According to the U.S. Department of Labor, computer and information systems managers had median annual earnings of $108,070 in 2007. Salaries ranged from less than $65,760 to more than $136,850.

Benefit and compensation packages for Internet executives are usually excellent and may include stock awards and options, cash incentives in addition to bonuses, company-paid insurance premiums, use of company cars, club memberships, expense accounts, and generous retirement benefits.

Top executives at successful Internet companies see few limits to their earnings potential; salaries into the millions of dollars are not uncommon for CEOs and other key executives.

WORK ENVIRONMENT

Internet executives often work in spacious offices with comfortable desks and chairs, computers, phones, and even personal support staff. On the other hand, some Internet companies may eschew private offices for their executives—instead placing them in common areas with their staffs to encourage creativity and collaboration.

Executives often travel between the company's various offices at the national, regional, or local levels. Top executives may travel to meet with executives in other corporations, both within the United States and abroad. They may also travel to trade shows and educational conferences. Executives who are employed by large national or multinational companies must be prepared to move for their work.

Executives often work long hours under intense pressure to meet corporate goals. A typical workweek might consist of 55 to 60 hours at the office. Some executives, in fact, spend up to 80 hours working each week. These long hours limit time available for family and leisure activities, but the financial rewards can be great.

OUTLOOK

Employment of Internet executives is expected to grow faster than the average over the next several years as Internet businesses continue to grow and new companies are formed. The demand will be high for candidates with strong managerial skills and a solid understanding of computer and Internet technology. Education and experience will also count for a lot. Many job openings will be the result of promotions, company expansions, or executives leaving their positions to start their own businesses.

The employment outlook for Internet executives is closely tied to the health of the computer and information technology industries, as well as the overall economy. When the economy is strong, businesses expand, which creates a need for more executives. In weak economic times, businesses often reduce their workforce and cut back on production, which lessens the need for executives.

There were many highly publicized dot-com failures in the early 2000s. Many experts predict that in the next few years, 80 to 90 percent of existing dot-coms will either close or be acquired by other companies. The statistics, however, are not likely to deter new Web businesses, especially small businesses that are able to find niche markets, anticipate trends, adapt to market and technology changes, and plan for a large enough financial margin to turn a profit. Traditional brick-and-mortar businesses will also have to implement dot-com marketing plans in order to compete and survive. Analysts anticipate that business-to-business e-commerce will become much more important than business-to-consumer transactions.

FOR MORE INFORMATION

For news about management trends, conferences, and seminars, visit the association's Web site.
American Management Association
1601 Broadway
New York, NY 10019-7434
Tel: 877-566-9441
http://www.amanet.org

To read about issues affecting chief information officers, visit
CIO.com
http://www.cio.com

There are a number of magazines covering the topics of the Internet, computers, and business. Many are available in print form and online. For a sampling of such magazines, check out the following Web sites:

Computerworld
http://www.computerworld.com

Information Week
http://www.informationweek.com

InfoWorld
http://www.infoworld.com

Macworld
http://www.macworld.com

PCWorld
http://www.pcworld.com

Wired
http://www.wired.com

For information on certification, contact
Institute for Certification of Computing Professionals
2350 East Devon Avenue, Suite 115
Des Plaines, IL 60018-4610
Tel: 800-843-8227
http://www.iccp.org

For information on certification, contact
Institute of Certified Professional Managers
James Madison University
MSC 5504
Harrisonburg, VA 22807-0001
Tel: 800-568-4120
http://icpm.biz

For information on programs that teach students about free enterprise and business and information on local chapters, contact
Junior Achievement
One Education Way
Colorado Springs, CO 80906-4477
Tel: 719-540-8000
Email: newmedia@ja.org
http://www.ja.org

For information on career opportunities in state government, contact
National Association of State Chief Information Officers
c/o AMR Management Services
201 East Main Street, Suite 1405
Lexington, KY 40507-2004
http://www.nascio.org

For general information on management careers, contact
National Management Association
2210 Arbor Boulevard
Dayton, OH 45439-1506
Tel: 937-294-0421
Email: nma@nma1.org
http://www.nma1.org

Labor Union Business Agents

OVERVIEW

Labor union business agents manage the daily business matters of labor unions and act as liaisons between the union and management during contract negotiations. They manage business affairs for the labor union that employs them and inform the media of labor union happenings. Labor union business agents are also responsible for informing employers of workers' concerns.

HISTORY

The idea of workers or craft workers banding together for their mutual benefit has existed for centuries. In the Middle Ages, groups such as blacksmiths and carpenters organized themselves into guilds, which established product and wage standards, set requirements for entering the trade, and erected barriers to outside competition. The first guilds in the United States were organized around the time of the Revolutionary War.

Unions were first organized in both England and the United States by workers in response to the industrial revolution of the 19th century. In 1886, the American Federation of Labor (AFL) was founded. Through collective bargaining tactics, the AFL was able to pass labor laws that gave workers higher wages, shorter hours, workers' compensation, and child labor laws. In the beginning of the 20th century, there was a huge growth in union membership, which jumped from less than 800,000 in 1900 to more than 5 million by 1920. Unionism got a further boost from such New Deal federal legislation as the Wagner Act in 1935, which established the National Labor Relations Board. In the same year, the Congress of Industrial Organizations (CIO) was created to bring about a separation between unions representing factory workers and those representing skilled craftspeople. The two groups eventually merged together, forming the AFL-CIO, which still exerts a powerful influence on improving working relations today.

Most unions are essentially organized into two types: the craft union, whose members are all skilled in a certain craft, such as carpentry or electrical work; and the industrial union, whose members work in the various jobs of a certain industry, such as automobiles or steel manufacturing. (Today, these two categories are not as clear cut because many professional workers, such as teachers and nurses, have also formed unions or been integrated into existing unions.) Companies began to reorganize around the existence of unions in the early 1900s. A company that hired only union members was called a "closed shop," while a "union shop" was one that required newly hired workers to join a union after a certain time period. The closed shop was outlawed in 1947 with the passage of the Taft-Hartley Act. Since then, more than one-third of the states have also outlawed the union shop by passing "right to work" laws, thereby weakening union power.

The economic recessions in the early 1980s and in more recent years caused further weakening of many unions' power, as employers in financially troubled industries asked unions for contract concessions in order to save the jobs of existing employees. In 2007 12.1 percent of wage and salary workers were represented by unions, according to the U.S. Department of Labor.

THE JOB

Union business agents act as representatives for the working members of the union, who are often called the "rank and file." Agents are usually elected by members in a democratic fashion, although sometimes they are appointed by the union's elected officers or executive board. A union agent normally represents a certain number of workers. In an industrial union, an agent could speak for workers in several small plants or a single large plant. In a craft union, an agent will represent a single trade or group of craft workers.

Unions are structured like corporations and government groups in many ways. In the same way that a company will follow the procedures described in its articles of incorporation to conduct meetings and elect its board of directors, a union follows the rules set down by its own constitution and democratically elects its leaders and representatives. Union leaders must be responsive to the wills of their union members, or they may be overruled in union meetings or defeated in their next bid for reelection. In industrial unions, local chapters are directed by a central union, which is led by a regional director and is part of a larger national or international union.

Craft unions are organized somewhat differently. A different business agent represents each craft, and several of these agents work on the staff of a district council. These district councils are like an organization of unions, each governed independently of the others, banding together for bargaining strength.

One of the most important aspects of a union business agent's job is the role as a liaison, or go-between, for workers and employers. This role becomes most apparent at the times when the union and its employers need to negotiate a new contract. The business agent needs to know what the members of the union want in order to talk with management about wages, benefits, pensions, working conditions, layoffs, workers' compensation, and other issues. The agent explains the union's position to management during pre-bargaining talks. During negotiations, the agent keeps the members informed of the progress of contract talks and advises them of management's position.

The business agent needs to be able to drive a hard bargain with employers while at the same time be aware of employer limitations so that an agreement can be reached that is suitable to all parties. If a contract agreement cannot be reached, a third party may be needed. *Conciliators*, or *mediators*, are dispute-resolution specialists who may be brought in to keep the talks moving on both sides. *Arbitrators*, sometimes called *referees* or *umpires*, help decide disputes by drawing up conditions that bind both workers and employers to certain agreements. Only as a last resort will labor union business agents help organize a general strike, which can hurt both labor and management financially. During a strike, workers are not paid and employers lose money from a loss in production.

In addition, the business agent is responsible for making certain that the union is serving its members properly. The agent often handles grievances expressed by union members and, if necessary, will work with people in the company to solve them. It is also the agent's job to make sure that employers carry out the terms of the union's contract. The agent is in constant contact with union members through the *shop steward*, who is the general representative for the union. The steward is either elected by the membership or appointed by the business agent.

Agents are also responsible for much of the public image of the union. This involves everything from contacting newspaper reporters and other members of the media to organizing charity drives. The business agent is often in charge of recruiting new members for the union, finding jobs for members who are out of work, conducting union meetings, and renting meeting halls.

REQUIREMENTS

High School
Union business agents should at least have a high school education. To build a solid background, take courses in business, English, mathematics, public speaking, history, and economics. If available, you should also take technical courses, such as shop and electronics.

Postsecondary Training
A college degree can also be valuable for union business agents. Many colleges now offer curricula in labor and industrial relations. Additional courses that you will also find useful include psychology, business, collective bargaining, labor law, occupational safety and health, economics, and political science. Some unions may offer to reimburse some of the costs of higher education for union members interested in leadership positions. In most cases, business agents will receive additional training on the job while working under experienced union leaders.

Other Requirements
To succeed as a union business agent, you need to have both relevant job skills and leadership qualities. Agents should have previous work experience in the trade, industry, or profession they represent in order to fully understand and appreciate the problems and concerns of the workers. Most business agents begin as industrial or craft workers, join a union, become involved in its affairs, and progressively move up through the ranks.

Agents must also possess leadership skills and be committed to the cause of the union and to the rights and concerns of the workers. Their role in negotiations requires intelligence, persuasiveness, self-discipline, and patience. They must be able to command the respect of both the employer and the members. A good command of the English language—both written and oral—is essential to articulate the concerns of the workers, understand the terms of union contracts, and persuade the representatives of the company and the union members to accept an agreement. If the union leadership has reached a decision that may be unpopular, the agent will have to explain the reasoning behind it to the members.

Facts About Unions, 2008

- 16.1 million people were members of unions in the United States—an increase of 428,000 from 2007.
- Education, training, and library workers (38.7 percent) had the highest unionization rates, followed by protective service workers (35.4 percent).
- Farming, fishing, and forestry workers (4.3 percent) and sales workers (3.3 percent) had the lowest unionization rates.
- Wage and salary workers ages 45 to 64 were much more likely to be members of a union than workers ages 16 to 24.
- Nearly 40 percent of public sector workers were members of unions; only 7.6 percent of private industry workers were union members.
- Union workers earned median weekly salaries of $886, while those who were not members of a union only earned $691 a week.
- New York, Alaska, and Hawaii had the highest percentage of union workers. North Carolina, Virginia, South Carolina, Georgia, and Texas had the lowest percentage of union workers.

Source: U.S. Department of Labor

EXPLORING

The career of labor union business agent offers you the opportunity to follow your career interest into such fields as teaching or electronics, and then expand as a leader of others. Whatever your specific interest area, you should also gain experience in policy making and hold positions of leadership to nurture the qualities necessary for a future career as a union business agent. Get involved with the student council, debate society, and other clubs with leadership opportunities. In addition, talking with working business agents can also lend insight into the daily responsibilities of union leadership.

EMPLOYERS

Since union business agents represent the workers in a labor union, they are employed by the various craft and industrial unions that normally represent a particular group of workers. There are active unions in nearly every line of work.

STARTING OUT

Almost all union business agents first work for a number of years in their respective industries and work their way up from the inside. Each type of industry has its own requirements for joining, such as previous experience, training, and apprenticeships. Once a member of a union, workers can seek out opportunities to become involved in union matters, such as serving on committees. Through efforts and dedication to the union's cause, workers attract the attention of union leadership, who may encourage them to run for a local union job in the next election. Initially, prospective agents are usually elected or appointed to the position of shop steward, who is responsible for communicating the members' wishes to the business agent. If popular and effective, the steward may then run for election as a union business agent. The process of electing or selecting representatives varies from union to union, but an agent usually serves a term of about three years.

ADVANCEMENT

A labor union business agent is in many ways like a politician. In the same ways that politicians can work their way from local to state government and possibly to Washington, D.C., union business agents can move upward in the ranks of leadership. If business agents do their jobs well, gain respect, and maintain high profiles, they may advance to positions at the council headquarters or at regional union offices. An experienced agent can even advance to represent the union at the international level.

EARNINGS

The earnings of business agents vary depending on the union's membership size and the type of business it represents. Agents' pay is usually prescribed in union bylaws or its constitution. Typically, their wages mirror the earnings of the highest-paid worker in the particular field the agent represents. Average starting salaries for agents are about $50,000. After five years' experience, business agents earn about $65,000, and after 10 years, $75,000 or more.

In addition, agents get the same benefits as other union members, such as paid holidays, health insurance, and pension plans. Some agents may drive a car owned by the union and have their expenses paid while they travel on union business.

WORK ENVIRONMENT

An agent's dedication to the union often dictates the amount of hours worked every week. Most agents work a 40-hour week, but often work much longer hours during contract bargaining talks and membership drives. They are also expected to be available 24 hours a day to handle any possible emergencies.

Agents generally split their time between office work at council or local headquarters, and fieldwork. They spend many hours visiting factories and construction sites, meeting with shop stewards, and listening to the opinions of the rank-and-file members. During these visits, they have to deal with the working conditions of their industry. Agents also travel a great deal and can be on the road for long periods of time.

OUTLOOK

The success of union business agents depends to a great extent on the strength and growth prospects of their particular unions as well as of their industries in general. The best opportunities for employment and advancement exist in those industries that are expected to grow in years to come.

In recent years there has been a strong shift in the U.S. economy away from manufacturing toward service industries. Such service industries include insurance, banking, legal services, health care, accounting, retailing, data processing, and education. According to the U.S. Department of Labor, the growth of these industries and the industries that support them will provide the greatest opportunities for unionization and union business agents through 2016. Unions already exist for public workers, such as teachers, police officers, and firefighters. Other opportunities for unionization and business agent employment will arise in health care, representing workers such as physicians, nurses, medical assistants, technicians, and custodians.

The manufacturing sector of the economy, which traditionally has been highly unionized, is expected to lose a large number jobs because of increasingly efficient technologies and competition from overseas. However, certain areas of opportunity will still exist in manufacturing. Increases are expected in pharmaceutical and medicine and aerospace product and parts manufacturing. The construction industry is also expected to show a steady increase in employment in the next decade.

FOR MORE INFORMATION

Following are a handful of national labor unions. For more detailed information about careers in a specific trade or profession, contact the appropriate local unions in your area.

American Federation of Labor and Congress of Industrial Organizations (AFL-CIO)
815 16th Street NW
Washington, DC 20006-4101
Tel: 202-637-5000
http://www.aflcio.org

American Federation of Teachers
555 New Jersey Avenue NW
Washington, DC 20001-2029
Tel: 202-879-4400
http://www.aft.org

International Association of Bridge, Structural, Ornamental, and Reinforcing Ironworkers
1750 New York Avenue NW, Suite 400
Washington, DC 20006-5301
Tel: 202-383-4800
http://www.ironworkers.org

International Union, United Automobile, Aerospace, and Agricultural Implement Workers of America
8000 East Jefferson Avenue
Detroit, MI 48214-3963
Tel: 313-926-5000
Email: uaw@uaw.org
http://www.uaw.org

United Steelworkers
Five Gateway Center
Pittsburgh, PA 15222-1214
Tel: 412-562-2400
http://www.usw.org

UNITE HERE
275 7th Avenue
New York, NY 10001-6708
Tel: 212-265-7000
http://www.uniteunion.org

Management Analysts and Consultants

OVERVIEW

Management analysts and consultants analyze business or operating procedures to devise the most efficient methods of accomplishing work. They gather and organize information about operating problems and procedures and prepare recommendations for implementing new systems or changes. They may update manuals outlining established methods of performing work and train personnel in new applications. There are approximately 678,000 management analysts and consultants employed in the United States.

HISTORY

During the industrial revolution, a number of people in business began experimenting with accepted management practices. For example, in the 1700s, Josiah Wedgwood applied new labor- and work-saving methods to his pottery business and was the first to formulate the concept of mass-producing articles of uniform quality. He believed the manufacturing process could be organized into a system that would use, and not abuse, the people harnessed to it. He organized the interrelationships between people, material, and events in his factory and took the time to reflect upon them. In short, he did in the 18th century what management analysts and consultants do today.

Frederick W. Taylor was the creator of the "efficiency cult" in American business. Taylor invented the world-famous "differential piecework" plan, in which a productive worker could significantly increase take-home pay by stepping up the pace of work. Taylor's well-publicized study of the Midvale Steel plant in Pennsylvania was the first time-and-motion study. It broke down elements of each part of each job and timed it, and Taylor was therefore able to quantify maximum efficiency. He earned many assignments and inspired James O. McKinsey, in 1910, to found a firm dealing with management and accounting problems.

Today, management analysts and consultants are thriving. As technological advances lead to the possibility of dramatic loss or gain in the business world, many executives feel more secure relying on all the specialized expertise they can find.

THE JOB

Management analysts and consultants are called in to solve any of a vast array of organizational problems. They are often needed when a rapidly growing small company needs a better system of control over inventories and expenses.

The role of the consultant is to come into a situation in which a client is unsure or inexpert and to recommend actions or provide assessments. There are many different types of management analysts and consultants. In general, they all require knowledge of general management, operations, marketing, logistics, materials management and physical distribution, finance and accounting, human resources, electronic data processing and systems, and management science.

Management analysts and consultants may be called in when a major manufacturer must reorganize its corporate structure when acquiring a new division. For example, they assist when a company relocates to another state by coordinating the move, planning the new facility, and training new workers.

The work of management analysts and consultants is quite flexible—it varies from job to job. In general, management analysts and consultants collect, review, and analyze data, make recommendations, and assist in the implementation of their proposals. Some projects require several consultants to work together, each specializing in a different area. Other jobs require the analysts to work independently.

Public and private organizations use management analysts for a variety of reasons. Some organizations lack the resources necessary to handle a project. Other organizations, before they pursue a particular course of action, will consult an analyst to determine what resources will be required or what problems will be encountered. Some companies seek outside advice on how to resolve organizational problems that have already been identified or to avoid troublesome problems that could arise.

Firms providing consulting practitioners range in size from solo practitioners to large international companies employing hundreds of people. The services are generally provided on a contract basis. A company will choose a consulting firm that specializes in the area that needs assistance, and then the two firms negotiate the conditions of the contract. Contract variables include the proposed cost of the project, staffing requirements, and the deadline.

After getting a contract, the analyst's first job is to define the nature and extent of the project. He or she analyzes statistics, such as annual revenues, employment, or expenditures. He or she may also interview employees and observe the operations of the organization on a day-to-day basis.

The next step for the analyst is to use his or her knowledge of management systems to develop solutions. While preparing recommendations, he or she must take into account the general nature of the business, the relationship of the firm to others in its industry, the firm's internal organization, and the information gained through data collection and analysis.

Once they have decided on a course of action, management analysts and consultants usually write reports of their findings and recommendations and present them to the client. They often make formal oral presentations about their findings as well. Some projects require only reports; others require assistance in implementing the suggestions.

REQUIREMENTS

High School

High school courses that will give you a general preparation for this field include business, mathematics, and computer science. Management analysts and consultants must pass on their findings through written or oral presentations, so be sure to take English and speech classes, too.

Postsecondary Training

Employers generally prefer to hire management analysts and consultants with a master's degree in business or public administration, or at least a bachelor's degree and several years of appropriate work experience. Many college majors provide a suitable education for this occupation because of the diversity of problem areas addressed by management analysts and consultants. These include many areas in the computer and information sciences, engineering, business and management, education, communications, marketing and distribution, and architecture and environmental design.

When hired directly from school, management analysts and consultants often participate in formal company training programs. These programs may include instruction on policies and procedures, computer systems and software, and management practices and principles. Regardless of their background, most management analysts and consultants routinely attend conferences to keep abreast of current developments in the field.

Certification or Licensing

The Institute of Management Consultants USA, in cooperation with the Association of Internal Management Consultants, offers the certified management consultant designation to those who pass an examination and meet minimum educational and experience criteria. Certification is voluntary, but may provide an additional advantage to job seekers.

Other Requirements

Management analysts and consultants are often responsible for recommending layoffs of staff, so it is important that they learn to deal with people diplomatically. Their job requires a great deal of tact, enlisting cooperation while exerting leadership, debating their points, and pointing out errors. Consultants must be quick thinkers, able to refute objections with finality. They also must be able to make excellent presentations.

A management analyst must also be unbiased and analytical, with a disposition toward the intellectual side of business and a natural curiosity about the way things work best.

EXPLORING

The reference departments of most libraries include business areas that will have valuable research tools such as encyclopedias of business consultants and "who's who" of business consultants. These books should list management analysis and consulting firms across the country, describing their annual sales and area of specialization, such as industrial, high tech, small business, or retail. After doing some research, you can call or write to these firms and ask for more information.

For more general business exploration, see if your school has a business or young leaders club. If there is nothing of the sort, you may want to explore Junior Achievement, a nationwide association that connects young business-minded students with professionals in the field for mentoring and career advice. Visit http://www.ja.org for more information.

EMPLOYERS

About 27 percent of the 678,000 management analysts and consultants in the United States are self-employed. Federal, state, and local governments employ many of the others. The Department of Defense employs the majority of those working for the federal government. The remainder of work is in the private sector for companies providing consulting services. Although management analysts and consultants are found throughout the country, the majority are concentrated in major metropolitan areas.

STARTING OUT

Most government agencies offer entry-level analyst and consultant positions to people with bachelor's degrees and no work experience. Many entrants are also career changers who were formerly mid- and upper-level managers. With 27 percent of the practicing management consultants self-employed, career changing is a common route into the field.

Anyone with some degree of business expertise or field of expertise can begin to work as an independent consultant: There are more than 100,000 one- and two-person consulting firms in this country. Establishing a wide range of appropriate personal contacts is by far the most effective way to get started in this field. Consultants have to sell themselves and their expertise, a task far tougher than selling a tangible product the customer can see and handle. Many consultants get their first clients by advertising in newspapers, magazines, and trade or professional periodicals. After some time in the field, word-of-mouth advertising is often the primary method of attracting new clients.

ADVANCEMENT

A new consultant in a large firm may be referred to as an *associate* for the first couple of years. The next progression is to *senior associate*, a title that indicates three to five years' experience and the ability to supervise others and do more complex and independent work. After about five years, the analyst who is progressing well may become an *engagement manager* with the responsibility to lead a consulting team on a particular client project. The best managers become *senior engagement managers,* leading several study teams or a very large project team. After about seven years, those who excel will be considered for appointment as *junior partners* or *principals.* Partnership involves responsibility for marketing the firm and leading client projects. Some may be promoted to senior partnership or *director,* but few people successfully run this full course. Management analysts and consultants with entrepreneurial ambition may open their own firms.

EARNINGS

Salaries and hourly rates for management analysts and consultants vary widely, according to experience, specialization, education, and employer. In 2007 management analysts and consultants had median annual earnings of $71,150, according to the U.S. Department of Labor. The lowest 10 percent earned less than $40,860, and the highest 10 percent earned more than $131,870.

Many consultants can demand between $400 and $1,000 per day. Their fees are often well over $40 per hour. Self-employed management consultants receive no fringe benefits and generally have to maintain their own office, but their pay is usually much higher than salaried consultants. They can make more than $2,000 per day; that can add up to $250,000 in one year from consulting just two days per week.

Typical benefits for salaried analysts and consultants include health and life insurance, retirement plans, vacation and sick leave, profit sharing, and bonuses for outstanding work. The employer generally reimburses all travel expenses.

WORK ENVIRONMENT

Management analysts and consultants generally divide their time between their own offices and the client's office or production facility. They can spend a great deal of time on the road.

Most management analysts and consultants work at least 40 hours per week plus overtime, depending on the project. The nature of consulting projects—working on location with a single client toward a specific goal—allows these professionals to totally immerse themselves in their work. They sometimes work 14- to 16-hour days, and six- or seven-day workweeks can be fairly common.

While self-employed, consultants may enjoy the luxury of setting their own hours and doing a great deal of their work at home; the trade-off is sacrificing the benefits provided by the large firms. Their livelihood depends on the additional responsibility of maintaining and expanding their clientele on their own.

Although those in this career usually avoid much of the potential tedium of working for one company all day, every day, they face many pressures resulting from deadlines and client expectations. Because the clients are generally paying generous fees, they want to see dramatic results, and the management analyst can feel the weight of this.

OUTLOOK

Employment of management analysts is expected to grow much faster than the average for all occupations through 2016, according to the U.S. Department of Labor. Industry and government agencies are expected to rely more and more on the expertise of these professionals to improve and streamline the performance of their organizations. Many job openings will result from the need to replace personnel who transfer to other fields or leave the labor force.

Competition for management consulting jobs will be strong. Employers can choose from a large pool of applicants who have a wide variety of educational backgrounds and experience. The challenging nature of this job, coupled with high salary potential, attracts many. A graduate degree, experience and expertise in the industry, as well as a knack for public relations, are needed to stay competitive.

Trends that have increased the growth of employment in this field include advancements in information technology and e-commerce, the growth of international business, and fluctuations in the economy that have forced businesses to streamline and downsize.

The U.S. Department of Labor predicts that opportunities will be best at very large consulting firms that have expertise in international business and in smaller firms that focus on providing consulting services in specific areas such as biotechnology, engineering, information technology, health care, marketing, and human resources.

FOR MORE INFORMATION

For industry information, contact the following organizations:
American Institute of Certified Public Accountants
1211 Avenue of the Americas
New York, NY 10036-8775
Tel: 212-596-6200
http://www.aicpa.org

American Management Association
1601 Broadway
New York, NY 10019-7434
Tel: 877-566-9441
http://www.amanet.org

Association of Management Consulting Firms
380 Lexington Avenue, Suite 1700
New York, NY 10168-0002
Tel: 212-551-7887
Email: info@amcf.org
http://www.amcf.org

For information on certification, contact
Association of Internal Management Consultants
824 Caribbean Court
Marco Island, FL 34145-3422
Tel: 239-642-0580
Email: info@aimc.org
http://www.aimc.org

For information on certification, contact
Institute of Management Consultants USA
2025 M Street NW, Suite 800
Washington, DC 20036-3309
Tel: 800-221-2557
Email: office@imcusa.org
http://www.imcusa.org

Office
Administrators

OVERVIEW

Office administrators direct and coordinate the work activities of office workers within an office. They supervise office clerks and other workers in their tasks and plan department activities with other supervisory personnel. Administrators often define job duties and develop training programs for new workers. They evaluate the progress of their clerks and work with upper management officials to ensure that the office staff meets productivity and quality goals. Office administrators often meet with office personnel to discuss job-related issues or problems, and they are responsible for maintaining a positive office environment. There are approximately 1.4 million office administrators employed in the United States.

HISTORY

The growth of business since the industrial revolution has been accompanied by a corresponding growth in the amount of work done in offices. Records, bills, receipts, contracts, and other paperwork have proliferated. Phone calls, emails, and other communications have multiplied. Accounting and bookkeeping practices have become more complicated.

The role of the office administrator has also grown over time. In the past, such supervisors were responsible mainly for ensuring productivity and good work from their clerks and reporting information to management. Today, office administrators play a more active part in the operations of busy offices. They are responsible for coordinating the activities of many departments, informing management of departmental performance, and making sure the highly specialized sectors of an office run smoothly and efficiently every day.

THE JOB

As modern technology and an increased volume of business communications become a normal part of daily business, offices are becoming more complicated places in which to work. By directing and coordinating the activities of clerks and other office workers, office administrators are an integral part of an effective organization.

The day-to-day work of office administrators, also known as *office managers,* involves organizing and overseeing many different activities. Although specific duties vary with the type and size of the particular office, all supervisors and managers have several basic job responsibilities. The primary responsibility of the office administrator is to run the office; that is, whatever the nature of the office's business, the office administrator must see to it that all workers have what they need to do their work.

Office administrators are usually responsible for interviewing prospective employees and making recommendations on hiring. They train new workers, explain office policies, and explain performance criteria. Office administrators are also responsible for delegating work responsibilities. This requires a keen understanding of the strengths and weaknesses of each worker, as well as the ability to determine what needs to be done and when it must be completed. For example, if a supervisor knows that one worker is especially good at filing business correspondence, that person will probably be assigned important filing tasks. Office administrators often know how to do many of the tasks done by their subordinates and assist or relieve them whenever necessary.

Office administrators not only train clerical workers and assign them job duties but also recommend increases in salaries, promote workers when approved, and, when necessary, fire them. Therefore, they must carefully observe clerical workers performing their jobs (whether answering the telephones, opening and sorting mail, or inputting computer data) and make positive suggestions for any necessary improvements. Managers who can communicate effectively, both verbally and in writing, will be better able to carry out this kind of work. Motivating employees to do their best work is another important component of an office administrator's responsibilities.

Office administrators must be very good at human relations. Differences of opinion and personality clashes among employees are inevitable in almost any office, and the administrator must be able to deal with grievances and restore good feelings among the staff. Office administrators meet regularly with their staff, alone and in groups, to discuss and solve any problems that might affect people's job performance.

Planning is a vital and time-consuming portion of the job responsibilities of office administrators. Not only do they plan the work of subordinates, they also assist in planning current and future office space needs, work schedules, and the types of office equipment and supplies that need to be purchased.

Office administrators must always keep their superiors informed as to the overall situation in the clerical area. If there is a delay on an important project, for example, upper management must know the cause and the steps being taken to expedite the matter.

REQUIREMENTS

High School

A high school diploma is essential for this position, and a college degree is highly recommended. You should take courses in English, speech and communications, mathematics, sociology, history, and as many business-related courses, such as typing and bookkeeping, as possible. Knowledge of a wide variety of computer software programs is also very important.

Postsecondary Training

In college, pursue a degree in business administration or at least take several courses in business management and operations. In some cases, an associate's degree is considered sufficient for a supervisory position, but a bachelor's degree will make you more attractive to employers and help in advancement.

Many community colleges and vocational schools offer business education courses that help train office administrators. The American Management Association has certificate programs in several areas, including administrative excellence, human resources, leadership, management excellence, and supervisory excellence. (See For More Information at the end of this article.)

Colleges and universities nationwide offer bachelor's degrees in business administration; a few may offer programs targeted to specific industries, such as medical administration or hotel management.

Certification or Licensing

The International Association of Administrative Professionals offers voluntary certification to administrative professionals. Applicants who meet experience requirements and who pass an examination may use the designation certified administrative professional. The Institute of Certified Professional Managers offers the certified manager designation to applicants who pass examinations that cover the foundations of management, planning and organizing, and leading and controlling.

Other Requirements

Offices can be hectic places. Deadlines on major projects can create tension, especially if some workers are sick or overburdened. Office administrators must constantly juggle the demands of their superiors with the capabilities of their subordinates. Thus, office administrators need an even temperament and the ability to work well with others. Other important attributes include organizational ability, attention to detail, dependability, and trustworthiness. Since many offices promote administrators from clerical work positions within their organization, relevant work experience is also helpful.

EXPLORING

You can get general business experience by taking on clerical or bookkeeping responsibilities with a school club or other organization. Volunteering in your school office is an ideal introduction to office work. This will allow you to become more familiar with computer programs often used in offices and practice business skills such as opening and sorting mail, answering telephones, and filing documents.

Community colleges and other institutions may offer basic or advanced computer training courses for students of all ages. After high school, you may want to explore work-study programs where you can work part time and gain on-the-job training with local businesses while earning your degree.

EMPLOYERS

Approximately 1.4 million office administrators are employed in the United States. Administrators are needed in all types of offices that have staffs large enough to warrant a manager. The federal government is a major employer of office administrators. Other job opportunities are found in private companies with large clerical staffs, such as banks, telecommunications companies, wholesalers, retail establishments, business service firms, healthcare facilities, schools, and insurance companies.

STARTING OUT

To break into this career, you should contact the personnel offices of individual firms directly. This is especially appropriate if you have previous clerical experience. College career services offices or other job placement offices may also know of openings. You can also locate jobs through help wanted advertisements. Another option is to sign up with a temporary employment service. Working as a "temp" provides the advantage of getting a firsthand look at a variety of office settings and making many contacts.

Often, a firm will recruit office administrators from its own clerical staff. A clerk with potential supervisory abilities may be given periodic supervisory responsibilities. Later, when an opening occurs for an administrator, that person may be promoted to a full-time position.

ADVANCEMENT

Skilled administrators may be promoted to group manager positions. Promotions, however, often depend on the individual's level of education and other appropriate training, such as training in the company's computer system. Firms usually encourage their employees to pursue further education and may even pay for some tuition costs. Supervisory and management skills can be obtained through company training or community colleges and local vocational schools.

Some companies will prepare office clerks for advancement to administrative positions by having them work in several company departments. This broad experience allows the administrator to better coordinate numerous activities and make more knowledgeable decisions.

EARNINGS

According to the U.S. Department of Labor, office administrators earned median annual salaries of $44,650 in 2007. Fifty percent earned between $34,540 and $57,700 per year. The lowest paid 10 percent earned less than $27,190, and the top paid 10 percent earned more than $73,000.

The size and geographic location of the company and the person's individual skills can be key determinants of earnings. Higher wages will be paid to those who work for larger private companies located in and around major metropolitan areas. Full-time workers also receive paid vacations and health and life insurance. Some companies offer year-end bonuses and stock options.

WORK ENVIRONMENT

As is the case with most office workers, office administrators work an average of 35 to 40 hours a week, although overtime is not unusual. Depending on the company, night, weekend, holiday, or shift work may be expected. Most offices are pleasant places to work. The environment is usually well ventilated and well lighted, and the work is not physically strenuous. The administrator's job can be stressful, however, as it entails supervising a variety of employees with different personalities, temperaments, and work habits.

OUTLOOK

Employment of office administrators is projected to grow more slowly than the average for all occupations through 2016, according to the U.S. Department of Labor. The increased use of data processing and other automated equipment as well as corporate downsizing may reduce the number of administrators in the next decade. However, this profession will still offer good employment prospects because of its sheer size. A large number of job openings will occur as administrators transfer to other industries or leave the workforce for other reasons. Since some clerical occupations will be affected by increased automation, some office administrators may have smaller staffs and be asked to perform more professional tasks.

The federal government should continue to be a good source for job opportunities. Private companies, particularly those with large clerical staffs, such as hospitals, banks, and telecommunications companies, should also have numerous openings. Employment opportunities will be especially good for those who are familiar with the latest computer technology and office equipment.

FOR MORE INFORMATION

For news about management trends, resources on career information and finding a job, and an online job bank, contact
American Management Association
1601 Broadway
New York, NY 10019-7434
Tel: 877-566-9441
http://www.amanet.org

For industry information, contact
Association of Professional Office Managers
1 Research Court, Suite 450

Rockville, MD 20850-6252
Tel: 866-738-3966
http://www.apomonline.org

For information on certification, contact
Institute of Certified Professional Managers
James Madison University
MSC 5504
Harrisonburg, VA 22807-0001
Tel: 800-568-4120
http://icpm.biz

For career and certification information, contact
International Association of Administrative Professionals
10502 NW Ambassador Drive
PO Box 20404
Kansas City, MO 64195-0404
Tel: 816-891-6600
http://www.iaap-hq.org

For information about programs for students in kindergarten through high school, and information on local chapters, contact
Junior Achievement
One Education Way
Colorado Springs, CO 80906-4477
Tel: 719-540-8000
Email: newmedia@ja.org
http://www.ja.org

For career information, contact
National Management Association
2210 Arbor Boulevard
Dayton, OH 45439-1506
Tel: 937-294-0421
Email: nma@nma1.org
http://www.nma1.org

Office Clerks

QUICK FACTS

School Subjects
Business
English
Mathematics

Personal Skills
Communication/ideas
Following instructions

Work Environment
Primarily indoors
Primarily one location

Minimum Education Level
High school diploma

Salary Range
$15,490 to $24,460 to $38,780+

Certification or Licensing
Voluntary

Outlook
About as fast as the average

DOT
209

GOE
09.07.02

NOC
1411

O*NET-SOC
43-9061.00

OVERVIEW

Office clerks perform a variety of clerical tasks that help an office run smoothly, including file maintenance, mail sorting, and record keeping. In large companies, office clerks might have specialized tasks such as inputting data into a computer, but in most cases, clerks are flexible and have many duties including typing, answering telephones, taking messages, responding to emails, making photocopies, and preparing mailings. Office clerks usually work under close supervision, often with experienced clerks directing their activities. There are approximately 3.2 million office clerks employed in the United States.

HISTORY

Before the 18th century, many businesspeople did their own office work, such as shipping products, accepting payments, and recording inventory. The industrial revolution changed the nature of business by popularizing the specialization of labor, which allowed companies to increase their output dramatically. At this time, office clerks were brought in to handle the growing amount of clerical duties.

Office workers have become more important as computers, word processors, and other technological advances have increased both the volume of business information available and the speed with which administrative decisions can be made. The number of office workers in the United States has grown as more trained personnel are needed to handle the volume of business communication and information. Businesses and government agencies depend on skilled office workers to file and sort documents, operate office equipment, and cooperate with others to ensure the flow of information.

THE JOB

Office clerks perform a variety of tasks as part of their overall job responsibilities. They may type or file bills, statements, and business correspondence. They may stuff envelopes, answer telephones, respond to emails, and sort mail. Office clerks also enter data into computers, run errands, and operate office equipment such as photocopiers, fax machines, and switchboards. In the course of an average day, an office clerk usually performs a combination of these and other clerical tasks, spending an hour or so on one task and then moving on to another as directed by an office manager or other supervisor.

An office clerk may work with other office personnel, such as a bookkeeper or accountant, to maintain a company's financial records. The clerk may type and mail invoices and sort payments as they come in, keep payroll records, or take inventories. With more experience, the clerk may be asked to update customer files to reflect receipt of payments and verify records for accuracy.

Office clerks often deliver messages from one office worker to another, an especially important responsibility in larger companies. Clerks may relay questions and answers from one department head to another. Similarly, clerks may relay messages from people outside the company or employees who are outside of the office to those working in house. Office clerks may also work with other personnel on individual projects, such as preparing a yearly budget or making sure a mass mailing gets out on time.

Administrative clerks assist in the efficient operation of an office by compiling business records; providing information to sales personnel and customers; and preparing and sending out bills, policies, invoices, and other business correspondence. Administrative clerks may also keep financial records and prepare the payroll. *File clerks* review and classify letters, documents, articles, and other information and then file this material so it can be quickly retrieved at a later time. They contribute to the smooth distribution of information at a company.

Some clerks have titles that describe where they work and the jobs they do. For example, *congressional-district aides* work for the elected officials of their U.S. congressional district. *Police clerks* handle routine office procedures in police stations, and *concrete products dispatchers* work with construction firms on building projects.

An office clerk sorts documents. *(Tony Savino/The Image Works)*

REQUIREMENTS

High School

To prepare for a career as an office clerk, you should take courses in English, mathematics, and as many business-related subjects as possible. Community colleges and vocational schools often offer business education courses that provide training for general office workers.

Postsecondary Training
A high school diploma is usually sufficient for beginning office clerks, although business courses covering office machine operation and bookkeeping are also helpful. To succeed in this field, you should have computer skills, the ability to concentrate for long periods of time on repetitive tasks, good English and communication skills, and mathematical abilities. Legible handwriting is also a necessity.

Certification or Licensing
The International Association of Administrative Professionals offers certification for administrative professionals (including office clerks). Contact the association for more information.

Other Requirements
To find work as an office clerk, you should have an even temperament, strong communication skills, and the ability to work well with others. You should find systematic and detailed work appealing. Other personal qualifications include dependability, trustworthiness, and a neat personal appearance.

EXPLORING

You can gain experience by taking on clerical or bookkeeping responsibilities with a school club or other organization. In addition, some school work-study programs may provide opportunities for part-time on-the-job training with local businesses. You may also be able to get a part-time or summer job in a business office by contacting businesses directly or by enlisting the aid of a guidance counselor. Training in the operation of business machinery (computers, word processors, and so on) may be available through evening courses offered by business schools and community colleges.

EMPLOYERS

Approximately 3.2 million office clerks are employed throughout the United States. Major employers include local government; utility companies; health care companies; finance and insurance agencies; real estate; professional, scientific, and technical services companies; and other large firms. Smaller companies also hire office workers and sometimes offer a greater opportunity to gain experience in a variety of clerical tasks.

STARTING OUT

To secure an entry-level position, you should contact businesses or government agencies directly. Newspaper ads, temporary-work agencies, online ads, and online job boards are also good sources for finding jobs in this area. Most companies provide on-the-job training, during which company policies and procedures are explained.

ADVANCEMENT

Office clerks usually begin their employment performing more routine tasks such as delivering messages and sorting and filing mail. With experience, they may advance to more complicated assignments and assume a greater responsibility for the entire project to be completed. Those who demonstrate the desire and ability may move to other clerical positions, such as secretary or receptionist. Clerks with good leadership skills may become group managers or supervisors. To be promoted to a professional occupation such as accountant, a college degree or other specialized training is usually necessary.

The high turnover rate that exists among office clerks increases promotional opportunities. The number and kind of opportunities, however, usually depends on the place of employment and the ability, education, and experience of the employee.

EARNINGS

Salaries for office clerks vary depending on the size and geographic location of the company and the skills of the worker. According to the U.S. Department of Labor (USDL), the median annual salary for full-time office clerks was $24,460 in 2007. The lowest paid 10 percent earned less than $15,490, while the highest paid group earned more than $38,780. The USDL reports that office clerks earned the following mean salaries by industry in 2007: local government, $28,650; general medical and surgical hospitals, $27,380; colleges, universities, and professional schools, $26,070; and elementary and secondary schools, $26,300. Full-time workers generally also receive paid vacations, health insurance, sick leave, and other benefits.

WORK ENVIRONMENT

As is the case with most office workers, office clerks work an average 40-hour week. They usually work in comfortable surroundings and are provided with modern equipment. Although clerks have a variety of tasks and responsibilities, the job itself can be fairly routine and repetitive. Clerks often interact with accountants and other office personnel and may work under close supervision.

OUTLOOK

Although employment of clerks is expected to grow only about as fast as the average for all careers through 2016, there will still be many jobs available due to the vastness of this field and a high turnover rate. With the increased use of data processing equipment and other types of automated office machinery, more and more employers are hiring people proficient in a variety of office tasks. According to OfficeTeam, the following industries show the strongest demand for qualified administrative staff: technology, financial services, construction, and manufacturing.

Because they are so versatile, office workers can find employment in virtually any kind of industry, so their overall employment does not depend on the fortunes of any single sector of the economy. In addition to private companies, the federal government should continue to be a good source of jobs. Office clerks with excellent computer skills, proficiency in office machinery, strong communication skills, and the ability to perform many tasks at once will be in strong demand. Temporary and part-time work opportunities should also increase, especially during busy business periods.

FOR MORE INFORMATION

For information on seminars, conferences, and news on the industry, contact
Association of Executive and Administrative Professionals
900 South Washington Street, Suite G-13
Falls Church, VA 22046-4009
Tel: 703-237-8616
Email: headquarters@theaeap.com
http://www.naesaa.com

For information on certification, contact
International Association of Administrative Professionals
10502 NW Ambassador Drive
PO Box 20404
Kansas City, MO 64195-0404
Tel: 816-891-6600
Email: service@iaap-hq.org
http://www.iaap-hq.org

For free office career and salary information, visit
OfficeTeam
http://www.officeteam.com

Personnel and Labor Relations Specialists

QUICK FACTS

School Subjects
Business
Psychology

Personal Skills
Communication/ideas
Leadership/management

Work Environment
Primarily indoors
One location with some
  travel

Minimum Education Level
Bachelor's degree

Salary Range
$27,360 to $54,280 to
  $120,960+

Certification or Licensing
Recommended

Outlook
Faster than the average

DOT
166

GOE
13.01.01, 13.02.01

NOC
1223

O*NET-SOC
11-3040.00, 11-3041.00,
  11-3042.00, 11-3049.00,
  13-1071.00, 13-1071.01,
  13-1071.02, 13-1072.00,
  13-1073.00, 13-1079.00,
  43-4111.00, 43-4161.00

OVERVIEW

Personnel specialists, also known as *human resources professionals*, formulate policy and organize and conduct programs relating to all phases of personnel activity. *Labor relations specialists* serve as mediators between employees and the employer. They represent management during the collective-bargaining process when contracts with employees are negotiated. They also represent the company at grievance hearings, which are required when a worker feels management has not fulfilled its end of an employment contract. There are approximately 868,000 personnel specialists employed in the United States.

HISTORY

The concept of personnel work developed as businesses grew in size from small owner-operated affairs to large corporate structures with many employees. As these small businesses became larger, it became increasingly difficult for owners and managers to stay connected and in touch with all their employees and still run the day-to-day operations of the business. Smart business owners and managers, however, were aware that the success of their companies depended upon attracting good employees, matching them to jobs they were suited for, and motivating them to do their best. To meet these needs, the personnel department was established, headed by a specialist or staff of specialists whose job was to oversee all aspects of employee relations.

The field of personnel, or human resources, grew as business owners and managers became more aware of the importance of human psychology in managing employees. The development of more sophisticated business methods, the rise of labor unions, and the enactment of government laws and regulations concerned with the welfare and rights of employees have all created an even greater need for personnel specialists who can balance the needs of both employees and employers for the benefit of all.

The development and growth of labor unions in the late 1700s and early 1800s created the need for a particular kind of personnel specialist—one who could work as a liaison between a company's management and its unionized employees. Labor relations specialists often try to arbitrate, or settle, employer-employee disagreements. One of the earliest formal examples of this sort of arbitration in the United States was the first arbitral tribunal created by the New York Chamber of Commerce in 1768. Although arbitration resolutions were often ignored by the courts in preindustrial United States, by the end of World War I, the court system was overwhelmed by litigation—and in 1925 the Federal Arbitration Act was passed, which enforced arbitration agreements reached independent of the courts. Today, personnel and labor relations workers are an integral part of the corporate structure to promote and communicate the needs of workers to management.

THE JOB

Personnel and labor relations specialists are the liaison between the management of an organization and its employees. They see that management makes effective use of employees' skills, while at the same time improving working conditions for employees and helping them find fulfillment in their jobs. Most positions in this field involve heavy contact with people, at both management and nonmanagement levels.

Both personnel specialists and labor relations specialists are experts in employer–employee relations, although the labor relations specialists concentrate on matters pertaining to union members. Personnel specialists interview job applicants and select or recommend those who seem best suited to the company's needs. Their choices for hiring and advancement must follow the guidelines for equal employment opportunity and affirmative action established by the federal government. Personnel specialists also plan and maintain programs for wages and salaries, employee benefits, and training and career development.

In small companies, one person often handles all the personnel work. This is the case for Susan Eckerle, human resources manager for Crane Federal Credit Union. She is responsible for all aspects of personnel management for 50 employees who work at three different locations. "I handle all hiring, employee relations counseling, corrective action, administration of benefits, and termination," she says. When Eckerle started working for the credit union, there was no specific human resources department. Therefore, much of her time is spent establishing policies and procedures to ensure that personnel matters run smoothly and consistently. "I've had to write job descriptions, set up interview procedures, and write the employee handbook," she says. "In addition, we don't have a long-term disability plan, and I think we need one. So I've been researching that."

Although Eckerle handles all phases of the human resources process, this is not always the case. The personnel department of a large organization may be staffed by many specialists, including recruiters, interviewers, and job analysts, as well as specialists in charge of benefits, training, and labor relations. In addition, a large personnel department might include *personnel clerks* and *assistants* who issue forms, maintain files, compile statistics, answer inquiries, and do other routine tasks.

Personnel managers and *employment managers* are concerned with the overall functioning of the personnel department and may be involved with hiring, employee orientation, record keeping, insurance reports, wage surveys, budgets, grievances, and analyzing statistical data and reports. *Industrial relations directors* formulate the policies to be carried out by the various department managers.

Of all the personnel specialists, the one who first meets new employees is often the recruiter. Companies depend on *personnel recruiters* to find the best employees available. To do this, recruiters develop sources through contacts within the community. In some cases, they travel extensively to other cities or to college campuses to meet with college placement directors, attend campus job fairs, and conduct preliminary interviews with potential candidates.

Employment interviewers interview applicants to fill job vacancies, evaluate their qualifications, and recommend hiring the most promising candidates. They sometimes administer tests, check references and backgrounds, and arrange for indoctrination and training. They must also be familiar and current with guidelines for equal employment opportunity (EEO) and affirmative action.

In very large organizations, the complex and sensitive area of EEO is handled by specialists who may be called *EEO representatives, affirmative-action coordinators,* or *job development specialists.* These specialists develop employment opportunities and on-the-job training programs for minority or disadvantaged applicants; devise systems or set up representative committees through which grievances can be investigated and resolved as they come up; and monitor corporate practices to prevent possible EEO violations. Preparing and submitting EEO statistical reports is also an important part of their work.

Job analysts are sometimes also called *compensation analysts* and *position classifiers.* They study all of the jobs within an organization to determine job and worker requirements. Through observation and interviews with employees, they gather and analyze detailed information about job duties and the training and skills required. They write summaries describing each job, its specifications, and the possible route to advancement. Job analysts classify new positions as they are introduced and review existing jobs periodically. These job descriptions, or position classifications, form a structure for hiring, training, evaluating, and promoting employees, as well as for establishing an equitable pay system.

Occupational analysts conduct technical research on job relationships, functions, and content; worker characteristics; and occupational trends. The results of their studies enable business, industry, and the government to utilize the general workforce more effectively.

Developing and administering the pay system is the primary responsibility of the *compensation manager.* With the assistance of other specialists on the staff, compensation managers establish a wage scale designed to attract, retain, and motivate employees. A realistic and fair compensation program takes into consideration company policies, government regulations concerning minimum wages and overtime pay, rates currently being paid by similar firms and industries, and agreements with labor unions. The compensation manager is familiar with all these factors and uses them to determine the compensation package.

Training specialists prepare and conduct a wide variety of education and training activities for both new and existing employees. Training specialists may work under the direction of an *education and training manager.* Training programs may cover such special areas as apprenticeship programs, sales techniques, health and safety practices, and retraining displaced workers. The methods chosen by training specialists for maximum effectiveness may include individual training, group instruction, lectures, demonstrations, meetings, or workshops, and using teaching aids such as handbooks, demonstration models, multimedia programs, and reference works. These specialists also confer with management and supervisors to determine the needs for new training programs or the revision of existing ones, maintain records of all training activities, and evaluate the success of the various programs and methods. Training instructors may work under the direction of an education and training manager. *Coordinators of auxiliary personnel* specialize in training nonprofessional nursing personnel in medical facilities.

Training specialists may help individuals establish career development goals and set up a timetable in which to strengthen job-related skills and learn new ones. Sometimes this involves outside study paid for by the company or rotation to jobs in different departments of the organization. The extent of the training program and the responsibilities of the training specialists vary considerably, depending on the size of the firm and its organizational objectives.

Benefits programs for employees are handled by *benefits managers* or *employee-welfare managers*. The major part of such programs generally involves insurance and pension plans. Since the enactment of the Employee Retirement Income Security Act (ERISA) in 1974, reporting requirements have become a primary responsibility for personnel departments in large companies. The retirement program for state and local government employees is handled by *retirement officers*. In addition to regular health insurance and pension coverage, employee benefit packages have grown to include such things as dental insurance, accidental death and disability insurance, automobile insurance, homeowner's insurance, profit sharing and thrift/savings plans, and stock options. The expertise of benefits analysts and administrators is extremely important in designing and carrying out the complex programs. These specialists also develop and coordinate additional services related to employee welfare, such as car pools, child care, cafeterias and lunchrooms, newsletters, annual physical exams, recreation and physical fitness programs, and counseling. Personal and financial counseling for employees close to retirement age is growing especially important.

In some cases—especially in smaller companies—the personnel department is responsible for administering the occupational safety and health programs. The trend, however, is toward establishing a separate safety department under the direction of a safety engineer, industrial hygienist, or other safety and health professionals.

Personnel departments may have access to resources outside the organization. For example, *employer relations representatives* promote the use of public employment services and programs among local employers. *Employee-health maintenance program specialists* help set up local government-funded programs among area employers to provide assistance in treating employees with alcoholism or behavioral medical problems.

In companies where employees are covered by union contracts, labor relations specialists form the link between union and management. Prior to negotiation of a collective-bargaining agreement, *labor relations managers* counsel management on their negotiating position and provide background information on the provisions of the current contract and the significance of the proposed changes. They also provide reference materials and statistics pertaining to labor legislation, labor market conditions, prevailing union and management practices, wage and salary surveys, and employee benefit programs. This work requires that labor relations managers be familiar with sources of economic and wage data and have an extensive knowledge of labor law and collective-bargaining trends. In the actual negotiation, the employer is usually represented by the director of labor relations or another top-level official, but the members of the company's labor relations staff play an important role throughout the negotiations.

Specialists in labor relations, or union-management relations, usually work for unionized organizations, helping company officials prepare for collective-bargaining sessions, participating in contract negotiations, and handling day-to-day labor relations matters. A large part of the work of labor relations specialists is analyzing and interpreting the contract for management and monitoring company practices to ensure their adherence to the terms. Of particular importance is the handling of grievance procedures. To investigate and settle grievances, these specialists arrange meetings between the workers who raise a complaint, the managers and supervisors, and a union representative. A grievance, for example, may concern seniority rights during a layoff. Labor relations disputes are sometimes investigated and resolved by *professional conciliators* or *mediators*. Labor relations work requires keeping up to date on developments in labor law, including arbitration decisions, and maintaining close contact with union officials.

Government personnel specialists do essentially the same work as their counterparts in business, except that they deal with public employees whose jobs are subject to civil service regulations. Much of government personnel work concentrates on job analysis, because civil service jobs are strictly classified as to entry requirements, duties, and wages. In response to the growing importance of training and career development in the public sector, however, an entire industry of educational and training consultants has sprung up to provide similar services for public agencies. The increased union strength among government workers has resulted in a need for more highly trained labor relations specialists to handle negotiations, grievances, and arbitration cases on behalf of federal, state, and local agencies.

REQUIREMENTS

High School
To prepare for a career as a personnel specialist or labor relations specialist, you should take high school classes that will help prepare you for college. A solid background in the basics—math, science, and English—should be helpful in college-level work. You might especially focus on classes that will help you understand and communicate easily with people. Psychology, English, and speech classes are all good choices. Business classes can help you understand the fundamental workings of the business world, which is also important. Finally, foreign language skills could prove very helpful, especially in areas where there are large numbers of people who speak a language other than English.

Postsecondary Training
High school graduates may start out as personnel clerks and advance to a professional position through experience, but such situations are becoming rare. Most employers require personnel specialists and labor relations specialists to have a college degree. After high school, Susan Eckerle attended a four-year college and received a bachelor's degree in retail management, with a minor in psychology. She says that if she were starting over now, however, she would get a degree in human resources instead.

There is little agreement as to what type of undergraduate training is preferable for personnel and labor relations work. Some employers favor college graduates who have majored in human resources, human resources administration, or industrial and labor relations, while others prefer individuals with a general business background. Another opinion is that personnel specialists should have a well-rounded liberal arts education, with a degree in psychology, sociology, counseling, or education. A master of business administration is also considered suitable preparation. Students interested in personnel work with a government agency may find it an asset to have a degree in personnel administration, political science, or public administration.

Individuals preparing for a career as a personnel specialist will benefit from a wide range of courses. Classes might include business administration, public administration, psychology, sociology, political science, and statistics. For prospective labor relations specialists, valuable courses include labor law, collective bargaining, labor economics, labor history, and industrial psychology.

Work in labor relations may require graduate study in industrial or labor relations. While not required for entry-level jobs, a law degree is a must for those who conduct contract negotiations, and a combination of industrial relations courses and a law degree is especially desirable. For a career as a professional arbitrator, a degree in industrial and labor relations, law, or personnel management is required.

Certification or Licensing

Some organizations for human resources professionals offer certification programs, which usually consist of a series of classes and a test. For example, the International Foundation of Employee Benefits Plans offers the certified employee benefit specialist designation to candidates who complete a series of college-level courses and pass exams on employee benefits plans. Other organizations that offer certification include the American Society for Training and Development, the Society for Human Resource Management, and WorldatWork Society of Certified Professionals. Although voluntary, certification is highly recommended and can improve chances for advancement.

Other Requirements

Personnel and labor relations specialists must be able to communicate effectively and clearly both in speech and in writing and deal comfortably and easily with people of different levels of education and experience. "You've got to be people oriented," says Eckerle. "You have to love people and like working with them. That is huge."

Objectivity and fair-mindedness are also necessary in this job, where you often need to consider matters from both the employee's and the employer's point of view. "Being the liaison between management and employees can put you in a tough spot sometimes," Eckerle says. "You're directly between the two poles, and you have to be able to work with both sides."

These workers cooperate as part of a team; at the same time, they must be able to handle responsibility individually. Eckerle says it is important to be organized because you are often responsible for tracking many different things regarding many different people. "You can't be sloppy in your work habits, because you're dealing with a lot of important information and it all has to be processed correctly," she says.

EXPLORING

If you enjoy working with others, you can find helpful experience in managing school teams, planning banquets or picnics, working in your dean's or counselor's office, or reading books about personnel practices in businesses. You might also contact and interview the personnel director of a local business to find out more about the day-to-day responsibilities of this job. Part-time and summer employment in firms that have a personnel department are very good ways to explore the personnel field. Large department stores usually have personnel departments and should not be overlooked as a source of temporary work.

EMPLOYERS

Personnel specialists hold approximately 868,000 jobs, with close to 90 percent working in the private sector. Of those specialists who work in the private sector, 13 percent work in administrative and support services; 10 percent work in professional, scientific, and technical services; 9 percent in finance and insurance firms; 9 percent in health care; and 7 percent in manufacturing. The companies that are most likely to hire personnel specialists are the larger ones, which have more employees to manage.

STARTING OUT

Colleges and universities have placement counselors who can help graduates find employment. Also, large companies that are looking for promising job applicants often send recruiters to campuses. Otherwise, interested individuals may apply directly to local companies.

While still in high school, you may apply for entry-level jobs as personnel clerks and assistants. Private employment agencies and local offices of the state employment service are other possible sources for work. In addition, newspaper want ads often contain listings of many personnel jobs.

Beginners in personnel work are trained on the job or in formal training programs, where they learn how to classify jobs, interview applicants, or administer employee benefits. Then they are assigned to specialized areas in the personnel department. Some people enter the labor relations field after first gaining experience in general personnel work, but it is becoming more common for qualified individuals to enter that field directly.

ADVANCEMENT

After trainees have mastered basic personnel tasks, they are assigned to specific areas in the department to gain specialized experience. In time, they may advance to supervisory positions or to manager of a major part of the personnel program, such as training, compensation, or EEO/affirmative action. Advancement may also be achieved by moving into a higher position in a smaller organization. A few experienced employees with exceptional ability ultimately become top executives with titles such as director of personnel or director of labor relations. As in most fields, employees with advanced education and a proven track record are the most likely to advance in human resources positions.

EARNINGS

Jobs for personnel specialists and labor relations specialists pay salaries that vary widely depending on the nature of the business and the size and location of the firm, as well as on the individual's qualifications and experience.

According to a survey conducted by the National Association of Colleges and Employers, an entry-level human resources specialist with a bachelor's degree in human resources, including labor and industrial relations, earned an annual salary of $41,680 in 2007.

The U.S. Department of Labor (USDL) reports that median annual earnings of human resources, training, and labor relations specialists were $54,280 in 2007. Salaries ranged from less than $27,360 to more than $91,180. The USDL reports the following mean annual salaries for human resources professionals by industry: federal government, $73,930; employment services, $56,660; local government, $54,400; and business, professional, labor, political, and similar organizations, $48,000. Human resources managers earned salaries that ranged from less than $54,250 to $120,960 or more in 2007.

Benefits for personnel and labor relations specialists depend on the employer; however, they usually include such items as health insurance, retirement or 401(k) plans, and paid vacation days.

WORK ENVIRONMENT

Personnel employees work under pleasant conditions in modern offices. Personnel specialists are seldom required to work more than 35 or 40 hours per week, although they may do so if they are developing a program or special project. The specific hours you work as a personnel specialist may depend upon which company you work for. "I work Monday through Friday," says Susan Eckerle, "but if you work for a company that has weekend hours, you'll probably have to work some weekends too. If you never work weekends, you won't know your employees."

Labor relations specialists often work longer hours, especially when contract agreements are being prepared and negotiated. The difficult aspects of the work may involve firing people, taking disciplinary actions, or handling employee disputes.

OUTLOOK

The U.S. Department of Labor (USDL) predicts that there will be faster than average growth through 2016 for human resources, training, and labor relations managers and specialists. The USDL predicts especially strong growth for training and development specialists and employment, recruitment, and placement specialists.

Competition for jobs will continue to be strong, however, as there will be an abundance of qualified applicants. Opportunities will be best in the private sector as businesses continue to increase their staffs as they begin to devote more resources to increasing employee productivity, retraining, safety, and benefits. Employment should also be strong with consulting firms that offer personnel and benefits and compensation services to business that cannot afford to have their own extensive staffs. As jobs change with new technology, more employers will need training specialists to teach new skills to their employees. Personnel specialist jobs may be affected by the trend in corporate downsizing and restructuring. Applicants who are certified will have the best prospects for employment.

FOR MORE INFORMATION

For information on standards and procedures in arbitration, contact
American Arbitration Association
1633 Broadway, 10th Floor
New York, NY 10019-6705
Tel: 212-716-5800
http://www.adr.org

For information on certification, contact
American Society for Training and Development
1640 King Street, Box 1443
Alexandria, VA 22313-1443

Tel: 703-683-8100
http://www.astd.org

For information about certification, contact
International Foundation of Employee Benefits Plans
PO Box 69
Brookfield, WI 53008-0069
Tel: 888-334-3327
http://www.ifebp.org

For information on training, job opportunities, and human resources publications, contact
**International Public Management Association for Human
    Resources**
1617 Duke Street
Alexandria, VA 22314-3406
Tel: 703-549-7100
http://www.ipma-hr.org

For general information on labor relations, contact
Labor and Employment Relations Association
University of Illinois—Urbana-Champaign
121 Labor and Industrial Relations Building
504 East Armory Avenue
Champaign, IL 61820-6221
Tel: 217-333-0072
Email: LERAoffice@illinois.edu
http://www.lera.uiuc.edu

For information on certification and to use an interactive career-mapping tool, visit the society's Web site.
Society for Human Resource Management
1800 Duke Street
Alexandria, VA 22314-3494
Tel: 800-283-SHRM
http://www.shrm.org

For news and information on compensation and benefits administration and certification, contact
WorldatWork
14040 North Northsight Boulevard
Scottsdale, AZ 85260-3601
Tel: 877-951-9191
http://www.worldatwork.org

INTERVIEW

Cathy Cortez is a senior labor relations manager for CN Railway, which has more than 20,400 route-miles of track in Canada and the United States. She has worked in the field for 10 years. Cathy discussed her career with the editors of Careers in Focus: Business.

Q. What are your primary and secondary job duties?

A. I work with union leaders and managers to help foster communication and negotiate collective bargaining agreements, which are the terms under which our unionized employees work.

When we cannot agree on interpretations or have a disagreement concerning the collective agreements, we proceed to arbitration. During arbitration, each party writes a submission detailing their side and presents that to a third-party neutral for a final decision.

Q. What do you like most and least about your job?

A. Most: the idea of new challenges every day and working with new people. More often than not, we're dealing with new situations that require debate, strategic thinking, and teamwork—not just working amongst us in the company, but working together with the union leaders to achieve a common goal.

Least: the adversarial aspect of some relationships. Obviously everyone doesn't agree on every point, every time. Working through those issues is difficult at times, and each side must remember that it's not personal when you don't agree.

Q. What advice would you give to high school students who are interested in this career?

A. Debate, speech team, writing courses, anything that would require freethinking and public speaking. It is also important to have good writing and research skills. The agreements and arbitration briefs must be put in proper form; both usually require some research.

Q. What is the most important professional quality for workers in your field?

A. Integrity. You cannot work with people, develop relationships, negotiate, and accomplish goals without that. You have to be true to your word and do what you say you're going to do.

Q. What is the employment outlook for your field?

A. As long as we have unions, there will be a need for labor and union relations.

Public Relations Specialists

OVERVIEW

Public relations (PR) specialists develop and maintain programs that present a favorable public image for an individual or organization. They provide information to the target audience (generally, the public at large) about the client, its goals and accomplishments, and any further plans or projects that may be of public interest.

PR specialists may be employed by corporations, government agencies, nonprofit organizations—almost any type of organization. Many PR specialists hold positions in public relations consulting firms or work for advertising agencies. There are approximately 243,000 public relations specialists in the United States.

HISTORY

The first public relations counsel was a reporter named Ivy Ledbetter Lee, who in 1906 was named press representative for coal mine operators. Labor disputes were becoming a large concern of the operators, and they had run into problems because of their continual refusal to talk to the press and the hired miners. Lee convinced the mine operators to start responding to press questions and supply the press with information on mine activities.

During and after World War II, the rapid advancement of communications techniques prompted firms to realize they needed professional help to ensure their messages were given proper public attention. Manufacturing firms that had

QUICK FACTS

School Subjects
Business
English
Journalism

Personal Skills
Communication/ideas
Leadership/management

Work Environment
Primarily indoors
One location with some
  travel

Minimum Education Level
Bachelor's degree

Salary Range
$29,580 to $49,800 to
  $94,620+

Certification or Licensing
Voluntary

Outlook
Faster than the average

DOT
165

GOE
01.03.01

NOC
5124

O*NET-SOC
11-2031.00, 27-3031.00

turned their production facilities over to the war effort returned to the manufacture of peacetime products and enlisted the aid of public relations professionals to forcefully bring products and the company name before the buying public.

Large business firms, labor unions, and service organizations such as the American Red Cross, Boy Scouts of America, and the YMCA, began to recognize the value of establishing positive, healthy relationships with the public that they served and depended on for support. The need for effective public relations was often emphasized when circumstances beyond the control of a company or institution created unfavorable reaction from the public.

Public relations specialists must be experts at representing their clients before the media. The rapid growth of the public relations field since 1945 is testimony to the increased awareness in all industries of the need for professional attention to the proper use of media and the proper public relations approach to the many publics of a firm or an organization—customers, employees, stockholders, contributors, and competitors.

THE JOB

Public relations specialists are employed to do a variety of tasks. They may be employed primarily as *writers,* creating reports, news releases, and booklet texts. Others write speeches or create copy for radio, television, or film sequences. These workers often spend much of their time contacting the press, radio, and television as well as magazines on behalf of the employer. Some PR specialists work more as *editors* than writers, fact-checking and rewriting employee publications, newsletters, shareholder reports, and other management communications.

Specialists may choose to concentrate in graphic design, using their background knowledge of art and layout to develop brochures, booklets, and photographic communications. Other PR workers handle special events, such as press parties, convention exhibits, open houses, or anniversary celebrations.

PR specialists must be alert to any and all company or institutional events that are newsworthy. They prepare news releases and direct them toward the proper media. Specialists working for manufacturers and retailers are concerned with efforts that will promote sales and create goodwill for the firm's products. They work closely with the marketing and sales departments in announcing new products, preparing displays, and attending occasional dealers' conventions.

A large firm may have a *director of public relations* who is a vice president of the company and in charge of a staff that includes writers, artists, researchers, and other specialists. Publicity for an individual or a small organization may involve many of the same areas of expertise but may be carried out by a few people or possibly even one person.

Many PR workers act as consultants (rather than staff) of a corporation, association, college, hospital, or other institution. These workers have the advantage of being able to operate independently, state opinions objectively, and work with more than one type of business or association.

PR specialists are called upon to work with the public opinion aspects of almost every corporate or institutional problem. These can range from the opening of a new manufacturing plant to a college's dormitory dedication to a merger or sale of a company.

Public relations professionals may specialize. *Lobbyists* try to persuade legislators and other office holders to pass laws favoring the interests of the firms or people they represent. *Fund-raising directors* develop and direct programs designed to raise funds for social welfare agencies and other nonprofit organizations.

Early in their careers, public relations specialists become accustomed to having others receive credit for their behind-the-scenes work. The speeches they draft will be delivered by company officers, the magazine articles they prepare may be credited to the president of the company, and they may be consulted to prepare the message to stockholders from the chairman of the board that appears in the annual report.

REQUIREMENTS

High School
While in high school, take courses in English, journalism, public speaking, humanities, and languages, because public relations is based on effective communication with others. Courses such as these will develop your skills in written and oral communication as well as provide a better understanding of different fields and industries to be publicized.

Postsecondary Training
Most people employed in public relations have a college degree. Major fields of study most beneficial to developing the proper skills are public relations, English, and journalism. Some employers feel that majoring in the area in which the public relations person will eventually work is the best training. A knowledge of business administration is also helpful, as is a natural talent for selling. A graduate degree may

be required for managerial positions. People with a bachelor's degree in public relations can find staff positions with either an organization or a public relations firm.

More than 200 colleges and about 100 graduate schools offer degree programs or special courses in public relations. In addition, many other colleges offer at least courses in the field. Public relations programs are sometimes administered by the journalism or communication departments of schools. In addition to courses in theory and techniques of public relations, interested individuals may study organization, management and administration, and practical applications and often specialize in areas such as business, government, and nonprofit organizations. Other preparation includes courses in creative writing, psychology, communications, advertising, and journalism.

Certification or Licensing
The Public Relations Society of America and the International Association of Business Communicators accredit public relations workers who have at least five years of experience in the field and pass a comprehensive examination. Such accreditation is a sign of competence in this field, although it is not a requirement for employment.

Other Requirements
Today's public relations specialist must be a businessperson first, both to understand how to perform successfully in business and to comprehend the needs and goals of the organization or client. Additionally, the public relations specialist needs to be a strong writer and speaker, with good interpersonal, leadership, and organizational skills.

EXPLORING

Almost any experience in working with other people will help you to develop strong interpersonal skills, which are crucial in public relations. The possibilities are almost endless. Summer work on a newspaper or trade paper or with a television station or film company may give insight into communications media. Working as a volunteer on a political campaign can help you to understand the ways in which people can be persuaded. Being selected as a page for the U.S. Congress or a state legislature will help you grasp the fundamentals of government processes. A job in retail will help you to understand some of the principles of product presentation. A teaching job will develop your organization and presentation skills. These are just some of the jobs that will let you explore areas of public relations.

Read More About It

Aronson, Merry, Don Spetner, and Carol Ames. *The Public Relations Writer's Handbook: The Digital Age.* 2d ed. San Francisco: Jossey-Bass, 2007.

Cohn, Robin. *The PR Crisis Bible: How to Take Charge of the Media When All Hell Breaks Loose.* Charleston, S.C.: BookSurge Publishing, 2008.

Meerman Scott, David. *The New Rules of Marketing and PR: How to Use News Releases, Blogs, Podcasting, Viral Marketing and Online Media to Reach Buyers Directly.* Hoboken, N.J.: Wiley, 2007.

Seitel, Fraser. *The Practice of Public Relations.* 10th ed. Upper Saddle River, N.J.: Prentice Hall, 2006.

Yaverbaum, Eric, Ilese Benun, and Bob Bly. *Public Relations For Dummies.* 2d ed. Hoboken, N.J.: For Dummies, 2006.

Zappala, Joseph M., and Ann R. Carden. *Public Relations Worktext: A Writing and Planning Resource.* Mahwah, N.J.: Erlbaum, 2004.

EMPLOYERS

Public relations specialists hold about 243,000 jobs. Workers may be paid employees of the organization they represent or they may be part of a public relations firm that works for organizations on a contract basis. Others are involved in fund-raising or political campaigning. Public relations may be done for a corporation, retail business, service company, utility, association, nonprofit organization, or educational institution.

Most PR firms are located in large cities that are centers of communications. New York, Chicago, San Francisco, Los Angeles, and Washington, D.C. are good places to start a search for a public relations job. Nevertheless, there are many good opportunities in cities across the United States.

STARTING OUT

There is no clear-cut formula for getting a job in public relations. Individuals often enter the field after gaining preliminary experience in another occupation closely allied to the field, usually some segment of communications, and frequently, in journalism. Coming into public relations from newspaper work is still a recommended route. Another good method is to gain initial employment as a public relations trainee or intern, or as a clerk, secretary, or research assistant in a public relations department or a counseling firm.

ADVANCEMENT

In some large companies, an entry-level public relations specialist may start as a trainee in a formal training program for new employees. In others, new employees may expect to be assigned to work that has a minimum of responsibility. They may assemble clippings or do rewrites on material that has already been accepted. They may make posters or assist in conducting polls or surveys, or compile reports from data submitted by others.

As workers acquire experience, they are given more responsibility. They write news releases, direct polls or surveys, or advance to writing speeches for company officials. Progress may seem to be slow, because some skills take a long time to master. Some workers advance in responsibility and salary in the same firm in which they started. Others find that the path to advancement is to accept a more attractive position in another firm.

The goal of many public relations specialists is to open an independent office or to join an established consulting firm. To start an independent office requires a large outlay of capital and an established reputation in the field. However, those who are successful in operating their own consulting firms probably attain the greatest financial success in the public relations field.

EARNINGS

Public relations specialists had median annual earnings of $49,800 in 2007, according to the U.S. Department of Labor. Salaries ranged from less than $29,580 to more than $94,620. The department reports the following 2007 mean salaries for public relations specialists by type of employer: advertising and related services, $65,030; business, professional, labor, political, and similar organizations, $62,080; management of companies and enterprises, $61,780; local government, $51,340; and colleges, universities, and professional schools, $48,640.

Many PR workers receive a range of fringe benefits from the corporations and agencies employing them, including bonus or incentive compensation, stock options, profit sharing, pension plans, 401 (k) programs, medical benefits, life insurance, financial planning, maternity/paternity leave, paid vacations, and family college tuition. Bonuses can range from 5 to 100 percent of base compensation and often are based on individual and/or company performance.

WORK ENVIRONMENT

Public relations specialists generally work in offices with adequate secretarial help, regular salary increases, and expense accounts. They are expected to make a good appearance in tasteful, conservative clothing. They must have social poise, and their conduct in their personal life is important to their firms or their clients. The public relations specialist may have to entertain business associates.

The PR specialist seldom works the conventional office hours; although the workweek may consist of 35 to 40 hours, these hours may be supplemented by evenings and even weekends during which meetings must be attended and other special events covered. Time behind the desk may represent only a small part of the total working schedule. Travel is often an important and necessary part of the job.

The life of the PR worker is so greatly determined by the job that many consider this a disadvantage. Because the work is concerned with public opinion, it is often difficult to measure the results of performance and to sell the worth of a public relations program to an employer or client. Competition in the PR field is keen, and if a firm loses an account, some of its personnel may be affected. The demands the career makes for anonymity will be considered by some as one of the profession's less inviting aspects. Public relations involves much more hard work and a great deal less glamour than is popularly supposed.

OUTLOOK

Employment of public relations professionals is expected to grow faster than the average for all occupations through 2016, according to the U.S. Department of Labor. Competition will be keen for beginning jobs in public relations because so many job seekers are enticed by the perceived glamour and appeal of the field; those with education and experience, as well as proficiency in one or more foreign languages, will have an advantage. The U.S. Department of Labor predicts that the advertising industry will offer the best employment opportunities for public relations specialists through 2016.

Most large companies have some sort of public relations resource, either through their own staff or through the use of a firm of consultants. They are expected to expand their public relations activities and create many new jobs. Growing numbers of smaller companies are hiring public relations specialists, adding to the demand for these workers. Additionally, as a result of recent corporate scandals, more public relations specialists will be hired to help improve the images of companies and regain the trust of the public.

FOR MORE INFORMATION

For information on program accreditation and professional development, contact
   Canadian Public Relations Society
   4195 Dundas Street West, Suite 346
   Toronto, ON M8X 1Y4 Canada
   Tel: 416-239-7034
   Email: admin@cprs.ca
   http://www.cprs.ca

For information on accreditation, contact
   International Association of Business Communicators
   601 Montgomery Street, Suite 1900
   San Francisco, CA 94111-2623
   Tel: 415-544-4700
   http://www.iabc.com

For statistics, salary surveys, and information on accreditation and student membership, contact
   Public Relations Society of America
   33 Maiden Lane, 11th Floor
   New York, NY 10038-5150
   Tel: 212-460-1400
   Email: prssa@prsa.org (student membership)
   http://www.prsa.org

Purchasing Agents

OVERVIEW

Purchasing agents work for businesses and other large organizations, such as hospitals, universities, and government agencies. They buy raw materials, machinery, supplies, and services required for the organization. They must consider cost, quality, quantity, and time of delivery. Purchasing agents hold approximately 303,000 jobs in the United States.

HISTORY

Careers in the field of purchasing are relatively new and came into real importance only in the last half of the 20th century. The first purchasing jobs emerged during the industrial revolution, when manufacturing plants and businesses became bigger. This led to the division of management jobs into various specialties, one of which was buying.

By the late 1800s, buying was considered a separate job in large businesses. Purchasing jobs were especially important in the railroad, automobile, and steel industries. The trend toward creating specialized buying jobs was reflected in the founding of professional organizations, such as the National Association of Purchasing Agents (now called the Institute for Supply Management) and the American Purchasing Society. It was not until after World War II, however, with the expansion of the U.S. government and the increased complexity of business practices, that the job of purchasing agent became firmly established.

QUICK FACTS

School Subjects
Business
Economics
Mathematics

Personal Skills
Helping/teaching
Technical/scientific

Work Environment
Primarily indoors
Primarily one location

Minimum Education Level
High school diploma

Salary Range
$27,810 to $52,460 to $86,860+

Certification or Licensing
Voluntary

Outlook
Little or no change

DOT
162

GOE
13.02.02

NOC
1225

O*NET-SOC
11-3061.00, 13-1021.00, 13-1023.00

THE JOB

Purchasing agents generally work for organizations that buy at least $100,000 worth of goods a year. Their primary goal is to purchase the best quality materials for the best price. To do this, the agent must consider the exact specifications for the required items, cost, quantity discounts, freight handling or other transportation costs, and delivery time. In the past, much of this information was obtained by comparing listings in catalogs and trade journals, interviewing suppliers' representatives, keeping up with current market trends, examining sample goods, and observing demonstrations of equipment. Increasingly, information can be found through computer databases, including those found on the Internet. Sometimes agents visit plants of company suppliers. The agent is responsible for following up on orders and ensuring that goods meet the order specifications.

Most purchasing agents work in firms that have fewer than five employees in their purchasing department. In some small organizations, there is only one person responsible for making purchases. Very large firms, however, may employ as many as 100 purchasing agents, each responsible for specific types of goods. In such organizations there is usually a purchasing director or purchasing manager.

Some purchasing agents seek the advice of *purchase-price analysts*, who compile and analyze statistical data about the manufacture and cost of products. Based on this information, they can make recommendations to purchasing personnel regarding the feasibility of producing or buying certain products and suggest ways to reduce costs.

Purchasing agents often specialize in a particular product or field. For example, *procurement engineers* specialize in aircraft equipment. They establish specifications and requirements for the construction, performance, and testing of equipment.

Field contractors negotiate with farmers to grow or purchase fruits, vegetables, or other crops. These agents may advise growers on methods, acreage, and supplies, and arrange for financing, transportation, or labor recruitment.

Head tobacco buyers are engaged in the purchase of tobacco on the auction warehouse floor. They advise other buyers about grades and quantities of tobacco and suggest prices.

Grain buyers manage grain elevators. They are responsible for evaluating and buying grain for resale and milling. They are concerned with the quality, market value, shipping, and storing of grain.

Grain broker-and-market operators buy and sell grain for investors through the commodities exchange. Like other brokers, they work on a commission basis.

REQUIREMENTS

High School

Most purchasing and buying positions require at least a bachelor's degree. Therefore, while in high school, take a college preparatory curriculum. Helpful subjects include English, business, mathematics, social sciences, and economics.

Postsecondary Training

Although it is possible to obtain an entry-level purchasing job with only a high school diploma, many employers prefer or require college graduates for the job, and the best jobs in government and at large companies go to those with a master's degree. College work should include courses in general economics, purchasing, accounting, statistics, and business management. A familiarity with computers also is desirable. Some colleges and universities offer majors in purchasing, but other business-related majors are appropriate as well.

Purchasing agents with a master's degree in business administration, public administration, engineering, technology, or finance tend to have the best jobs and highest salaries. Companies that manufacture machinery or chemicals may require a degree in engineering or a related field. A civil service examination is required for employment in government purchasing positions.

Certification or Licensing

There are no specific licenses or certification requirements imposed by law for purchasing agents. There are, however, several professional organizations to which many purchasing agents belong, including the Institute for Supply Management, the National Institute of Governmental Purchasing, APICS—The Association for Operations Management, and the American Purchasing Society. These organizations offer certification to applicants who meet their educational and other requirements and who pass the necessary examinations.

The Institute for Supply Management offers the accredited purchasing practitioner, certified purchasing manager, and certified professional in supply management designations. The National Institute of Governmental Purchasing and the Universal Public Purchasing Certification Council offer the certified public purchasing officer and the certified professional public buyer designations. APICS offers several certifications, including the certified supply chain professional designation. The American Purchasing Society offers the certified purchasing professional and certified professional purchasing manager designations. Although certification is not essential, it is a recognized mark of professional competence that enhances a purchasing agent's opportunities for promotion to top management positions.

Other Requirements

Purchasing agents should have calm temperaments and have confidence in their decision-making abilities. Because they work with other people, they need to be diplomatic, tactful, and cooperative. A thorough knowledge of business practices and an understanding of the needs and activities of the employer are essential, as is knowledge of the relevant markets. It also is helpful to be familiar with social and economic changes in order to predict the amounts or types of products to buy.

EXPLORING

If you are interested in becoming a purchasing agent, you can learn more about the field through a summer job in the purchasing department of a business. Even working as a stock clerk can offer some insight into the job of purchasing agent or buyer. You may also learn about the job by talking with an experienced purchasing agent or reading publications on the field such as *Purchasing* magazine (http://www.purchasing.com). Keeping abreast of economic trends, fashion styles, or other indicators may help you to predict the market for particular products. Making educated and informed predictions is a basic part of any buying job.

EMPLOYERS

There are approximately 303,000 purchasing agents (wholesale, retail, farm products, and other) currently working in the United States. They work for a wide variety of businesses, both wholesale and retail, as well as for government agencies. Employers range from small stores, where buying may be only one function of a manager's job, to multinational corporations, where a buyer may specialize in one type of item and buy in enormous quantity. Nearly every business that sells products requires someone to purchase the goods to be sold. These businesses are located nearly everywhere there is a community of people, from small towns to large cities. Of course, the larger the town or city, the more businesses and thus more buying positions. Larger cities provide the best opportunities for higher salaries and advancement.

STARTING OUT

Students without a college degree may be able to enter the field as clerical workers and then receive on-the-job training in purchasing. A college degree is required for most higher positions, however. College and university career services offices offer assistance to graduating students in locating jobs.

Entry into the purchasing department of a private business can be made by direct application to the company. Some purchasing agents start in another department, such as accounting, shipping, or receiving, and transfer to purchasing when an opportunity arises. Many large companies send newly hired agents through orientation programs, where they learn about goods and services, suppliers, and purchasing methods.

Another means of entering the field is through the military. Service in the Quartermaster Corps of the Army or the procurement divisions of the Navy or Air Force can provide excellent preparation either for a civilian job or a career position in the service.

ADVANCEMENT

In general, purchasing agents begin by becoming familiar with departmental procedures, such as keeping inventory records, filling out forms to initiate new purchases, checking purchase orders, and dealing with vendors. With more experience, they gain responsibility for selecting vendors and purchasing products. Agents may become junior buyers of standard catalog items, assistant buyers, or managers, perhaps with overall responsibility for purchasing, warehousing, traffic, and related functions. The top positions are head of purchasing, purchasing director, materials manager, and vice-president of purchasing. These positions include responsibilities concerning production, planning, and marketing.

Many agents advance by changing employers. Frequently an assistant purchasing agent will move up the career ladder by taking a job as a purchasing agent or head of the purchasing department at another company.

EARNINGS

How much a purchasing agent earns depends on various factors, including the employer's sales volume. Mass merchandisers, such as discount or chain department stores, pay among the highest salaries. According to 2007 U.S. Department of Labor data, annual earnings for purchasing agents (except wholesale, retail, and farm products) ranged from less than $32,580 for the lowest 10 percent to more than $86,860 for the top 10 percent. The median salary was $52,460. Wholesale and retail buyers (except farm products) had median earnings of $46,960 in 2007. Their salaries ranged from less than $27,810 to $86,660 or more annually. Purchasing agents and buyers of farm products had median annual earnings of $48,410 in 2007.

In addition to their salaries, buyers often receive cash bonuses based on performance and may be offered incentive plans, such as profit sharing and stock options. Most buyers receive the usual company benefits, such as vacation, sick leave, life and health insurance, and pension plans. They generally also receive an employee's discount of 10 to 20 percent on merchandise purchased for personal use.

WORK ENVIRONMENT

Working conditions for a purchasing agent are similar to those of other office employees. They usually work in rooms that are pleasant, well lighted, and clean. Work is year-round and generally steady because it is not particularly influenced by seasonal factors. Most have 40-hour workweeks, although overtime is not uncommon. In addition to regular hours, agents may have to attend meetings, read and prepare reports, visit suppliers' plants, or travel. While most work is done indoors, some agents occasionally need to inspect goods outdoors or in warehouses.

It is important for purchasing agents to have good working relations with others. They must interact closely with suppliers as well as with personnel in other departments of the company. Because of the importance of their decisions, purchasing agents sometimes work under great pressure.

OUTLOOK

Little or no employment change is expected for purchasing agents through 2016, according to the U.S. Department of Labor. (However, employment for purchasing agents of farm products is expected to decline through 2016 as a result of consolidation in the agricultural industry.) Computerized purchasing methods and the increased reliance on a select number of suppliers boost the productivity of purchasing personnel and have somewhat reduced the number of new job openings. But as more and more hospitals, schools, state and local governments, and other service-related organizations turn to professional purchasing agents to help reduce costs, they will become good sources of employment. Nevertheless, most job openings will replace workers who retire or otherwise leave their jobs.

Demand will be strongest for those with a master of business administration or an undergraduate degree in purchasing. Among firms that manufacture complex machinery, chemicals, and other technical products, the demand will be for graduates with a master's degree in engineering, another field of science, or business administration. Graduates of two-year programs in purchasing or materials management should continue to find good opportunities, especially in smaller companies.

FOR MORE INFORMATION

For career and certification information, contact
American Purchasing Society
PO Box 256
Aurora, IL 60506-0256
Tel: 630-859-0250
Email: propurch@propurch.com
http://www.american-purchasing.com

For information on certification, contact
APICS-The Association for Operations Management
8430 West Bryn Mawr Avenue, Suite 1000
Chicago, IL 60631-3439
Tel: 800-444-2742
http://www.apics.org

For career and certification information and lists of colleges with purchasing programs, contact
Institute for Supply Management
PO Box 22160
Tempe, AZ 85285-2160
Tel: 800-888-6276
http://www.ism.ws

For information on certification and purchasing careers in government, contact
National Institute of Governmental Purchasing
151 Spring Street
Herndon, VA 20170-5223
Tel: 800-367-6447
http://www.nigp.org

For materials on educational programs in the retail industry, contact
National Retail Federation
325 7th Street NW, Suite 1100
Washington, DC 20004-2808
Tel: 800-673-4692
http://www.nrf.com

Receptionists

OVERVIEW

Receptionists—so named because they receive visitors in places of business—have the important job of giving a business's clients and visitors a positive first impression. These front-line workers are the first communication sources who greet clients and visitors, answer their questions, and direct them to the people they wish to see. Receptionists also answer telephones, take and distribute messages for other employees, and make sure no one enters the office unescorted or unauthorized. Many receptionists perform additional clerical duties. *Switchboard operators* perform similar tasks but primarily handle equipment that receives an organization's telephone calls. There are approximately 1.2 million receptionists employed throughout the United States.

HISTORY

In the 18th and 19th centuries merchants and other businesspeople began to recognize the importance of giving customers the immediate impression that the business was friendly, efficient, and trustworthy. These businesses began to employ hosts and hostesses, workers who would greet customers, make them comfortable, and often serve them refreshments while they waited or did business with the owner. As businesses grew larger and more diverse, these hosts and hostesses (only recently renamed receptionists) took on the additional duties of answering phones, keeping track of workers, and directing visitors to the employee they needed to see. Receptionists also began to work as information dispensers, answering growing numbers of inquiries from the public. In

QUICK FACTS

School Subjects
Business
Computer science
English

Personal Skills
Communication/ideas
Following instructions

Work Environment
Primarily indoors
Primarily one location

Minimum Education Level
High school diploma

Salary Range
$16,290 to $23,710 to
$34,470+

Certification or Licensing
None available

Outlook
Faster than the average

DOT
237

GOE
09.05.01

NOC
1414

O*NET-SOC
43-4171.00

the medical field, for example, as services expanded, more reception-ists were needed to direct patients to physicians and clinical services and to keep track of appointments and payment information.

Soon receptionists became indispensable to business and service establishments. Today, it is hard to imagine most medium-sized or large businesses functioning without a receptionist.

A receptionist at a medical center interacts with a patient. *(Artiga Photo/ Corbis)*

THE JOB

The receptionist is a specialist in human contact: The most important part of a receptionist's job is dealing with people in a courteous and effective manner. Receptionists greet customers, clients, patients, and salespeople, take their names, and determine the nature of their business and the person they wish to see. The receptionist then pages the requested person and directs the visitor to that person's office or location, or makes an appointment for a later visit. Receptionists often keep records of all visits by writing down the visitor's name, purpose of visit, person visited, and date and time.

Most receptionists answer the telephone at their place of employment; many operate switchboards or paging systems. These workers usually take and distribute messages for other employees and may receive and distribute mail. Receptionists may perform a variety of other clerical duties, including keying in and filing correspondence and other paperwork, proofreading, preparing travel vouchers, and preparing outgoing mail. In some businesses, receptionists are responsible for monitoring the attendance of other employees. In businesses where employees are frequently out of the office on assignments, receptionists may keep track of their whereabouts to ensure they receive important phone calls and messages. Many receptionists use computers and word processors to perform clerical duties.

Receptionists are partially responsible for maintaining office security, especially in large firms. They may require all visitors to sign in and out and carry visitors' passes during their stay. Since visitors may not enter most offices unescorted, receptionists usually accept and sign for packages and other deliveries.

Receptionists are frequently responsible for answering inquiries from the public about a business's nature and operations. To answer these questions efficiently and in a manner that conveys a favorable impression, a receptionist must be as knowledgeable as possible about the business's products, services, policies, and practices and familiar with the names and responsibilities of all other employees. They must be careful, however, not to divulge classified information such as business procedures or employee activities that a competing company might be able to use. This part of a receptionist's job is so important that some businesses call their receptionists *information clerks*.

A large number of receptionists work in physicians' and dentists' offices, hospitals, clinics, and other health care establishments. Workers in medical offices receive patients, take their names, and escort them to examination rooms. They make future appointments for patients and may prepare statements and collect bill payments.

In hospitals, receptionists obtain patient information, assign patients to rooms, and keep records on the dates they are admitted and discharged.

In other types of industries, the duties of these workers vary. Receptionists in hair salons arrange appointments for clients and may escort them to stylists' stations. Workers in bus or train companies answer inquiries about departures, arrivals, and routes. In-file operators collect and distribute credit information to clients for credit purposes. Registrars, park aides, and tourist-information assistants may be employed as receptionists at public or private facilities. Their duties may include keeping a record of the visitors entering and leaving the facility, as well as providing information on services that the facility provides. Information clerks, automobile club information clerks, and referral-and-information aides provide answers to questions by telephone or in person from both clients and potential clients and keep a record of all inquiries.

Switchboard operators may perform specialized work, such as operating switchboards at police district offices to take calls for assistance from citizens. Or, they may handle airport communication systems, which includes public address paging systems and courtesy telephones, or serve as answering-service operators, who record and deliver messages for clients who cannot be reached by telephone.

REQUIREMENTS

High School
You can prepare for a receptionist position by taking courses in business, math, English, and public speaking. You should also take computer science courses.

Postsecondary Training
Most employees require receptionists to have a high school diploma. Some businesses prefer to hire workers who have completed post-high school courses at a junior college or business school. Courses in basic bookkeeping and principles of accounting will be helpful. This type of training may lead to a higher-paying receptionist job and a better chance for advancement. Many employers require typing, switchboard, computer, and other clerical skills, but they may provide some on-the-job training as the work is typically entry level.

Other Requirements
To be a good receptionist, you must be well-groomed, have a pleasant voice, and be able to express yourself clearly. Because you may

Employment/Earnings for Receptionists by Industry, 2007

Employer	# Employed	Annual Mean Earnings
Offices of physicians	173,550	$25,080
Offices of dentists	61,180	$27,850
Employment services	58,350	$23,850
Personal care services	56,320	$19,860
Offices of other health practitioners	40,400	$23,470

Source: U.S. Department of Labor

sometimes deal with demanding people, a smooth, patient disposition and good judgment are important. All receptionists need to be courteous and tactful. A good memory for faces and names also proves valuable. Most important are good listening and communications skills and an understanding of human nature.

EXPLORING

A good way to obtain experience as a receptionist is through a high school work-study program. Students participating in such programs spend part of their school day in classes and the rest working for local businesses. This arrangement will help you gain valuable practical experience before you look for your first job. High school guidance counselors can provide information about work-study opportunities.

EMPLOYERS

According to the U.S. Department of Labor, approximately 1.2 million people are employed as receptionists. Factories, wholesale and retail stores, and service providers employ a large percentage of these workers. Approximately 33 percent of the receptionists in the United States work in health care settings, including offices, hospitals, nursing homes, urgent care centers, and clinics. More than 30 percent work part time.

STARTING OUT

While you are in high school, you may be able to learn of openings with local businesses through your school guidance counselors or newspaper want ads. Local state employment offices frequently have information about receptionist work. You should also contact area businesses for whom you would like to work; many available positions are not advertised in the paper because they are filled so quickly. Temporary agencies are a valuable resource for finding jobs.

ADVANCEMENT

Advancement opportunities are limited for receptionists, especially in small offices. The more clerical skills and education workers have, the greater their chances for promotion to such better paying jobs as secretary, administrative assistant, or bookkeeper. College or business school training can help receptionists advance to higher-level positions. Many companies provide training for their receptionists and other employees, helping workers gain skills for job advancement.

EARNINGS

Earnings for receptionists vary widely with the education and experience of the worker and type, size, and geographic location of the business. The U.S. Department of Labor reported that in 2007, the median salary for receptionists was $23,710. The lowest paid 10 percent of these workers made less than $16,290 annually, while the highest paid 10 percent earned more than $34,470 per year. Receptionists are usually eligible for paid holidays and vacations, sick leave, medical and life insurance coverage, and a retirement plan of some kind.

WORK ENVIRONMENT

Receptionists usually work near or at the main entrance to the business. Therefore, these areas are usually pleasant and clean and are carefully furnished and decorated to create a favorable, businesslike impression. Work areas are almost always air-conditioned, well lit, and relatively quiet, although a receptionist's phone rings frequently. Receptionists work behind a desk or counter and spend most of their workday sitting, although some standing and walking is required when filing or escorting visitors to their destinations. The job may be stressful at times, especially when a worker must be polite to rude callers.

Most receptionists work five days, 35 to 40 hours per week. Some may work weekend and evening hours, especially those in medical offices. Switchboard operators may have to work any shift of the day if their employers (such as hotels and hospitals) require 24-hour phone service. These workers usually work holidays and weekend hours.

OUTLOOK

Employment for receptionists is expected to grow faster than the average for all careers through 2016, according to the *Occupational Outlook Handbook*. Many openings will occur due to the occupation's high turnover rate. Opportunities will be best for those with work experience and a variety of clerical skills. Growth in jobs for receptionists is expected to be greater than for other clerical positions because automation will have little effect on the receptionist's largely interpersonal duties and because of an anticipated growth in the number of businesses providing services. In addition, more and more businesses know how a receptionist can convey a positive public image. Opportunities should be especially good in physician's offices, law firms, temporary help agencies, and management and technical consulting firms.

FOR MORE INFORMATION

For information on careers, contact
International Association of Administrative Professionals
PO Box 20404
Kansas City, MO 64195-0404
Tel: 816-891-6600
Email: service@iaap-hq.org
http://www.iaap-hq.org

For free office career and salary information, visit
OfficeTeam
http://www.officeteam.com

Secretaries

QUICK FACTS

School Subjects
Business
Computer science
English

Personal Skills
Communication/ideas
Following instructions

Work Environment
Primarily indoors
Primarily one location

Minimum Education Level
High school diploma

Salary Range
$17,920 to $28,220 to
$60,800+

Certification or Licensing
Voluntary

Outlook
About as fast as the average

DOT
201

GOE
09.02.02

NOC
1241

O*NET-SOC
43-6012.00, 43-6013.00,
43-6014.00

OVERVIEW

Secretaries, or *administrative assistants*, perform a wide range of jobs that vary greatly from business to business. However, most secretaries key in documents, manage records and information, answer telephones, send and respond to emails and faxes, handle correspondence, schedule appointments, make travel arrangements, and sort mail. The amount of time secretaries spend on these duties depends on the size and type of the office as well as on their own job training. There are approximately 4.2 million secretaries employed in the United States.

HISTORY

People have always needed to communicate with one another for societies to function efficiently. Today, as in the past, secretaries play an important role in keeping lines of communication open. Before there were telephones, messages were transmitted by hand, often from the secretary of one party to the secretary of the receiving party. Their trustworthiness was valued because lives of many people often hung in the balance of certain communications.

Secretaries in the ancient world developed methods of taking abbreviated notes so that they could capture as much as possible of their employers' words. The modern precursors of the shorthand methods we know today developed in 16th-century England. In the 19th century, Isaac Pitman and John Robert Gregg developed the shorthand systems that are still used in offices and courtrooms in the United States.

The equipment secretaries use in their work has changed drastically in recent years. Almost every office, from the smallest to the largest, is automated in some way. Familiarity with machines including switchboards, photocopiers, fax machines, videoconferencing and telephone

Secretaries must have excellent communication skills. They frequently use the telephone to communicate with managers and coworkers. (*Jeff Greenberg/The Image Works*)

systems, scanners, and personal computers has become an integral part of the secretary's day-to-day work.

THE JOB

Secretaries perform a variety of administrative and clerical duties. The goal of all their activities is to assist their employers in the execution of their work and to help their companies conduct business in an efficient and professional manner.

Secretaries' work includes processing and transmitting information to the office staff and to other organizations. They operate office machines and arrange for their repair or servicing. These machines include computers, typewriters, dictating machines, photocopiers, switchboards, and fax machines. These secretaries also order office supplies and perform regular duties such as answering phones, sorting mail, managing files, taking dictation, and composing and keying in letters.

Some offices have word processing centers that handle all of the firm's typing. In such a situation, *administrative secretaries* take care of all secretarial duties except for typing and dictation. This arrangement leaves them free to respond to correspondence, prepare reports, do research and present the results to their employers, and otherwise assist the professional staff. Often these secretaries work in groups of three or four so that they can help each other if one secretary has a workload that is heavier than normal.

In many offices, secretaries make appointments for company executives and keep track of the office schedule. They make travel arrangements for the professional staff or for clients, and occasionally are asked to travel with staff members on business trips. Other secretaries might manage the office while their supervisors are away on vacation or business trips.

Secretaries take minutes at meetings, write up reports, and compose and type letters. They often will find their responsibilities growing as they learn the business. Some are responsible for finding speakers for conferences, planning receptions, and arranging public relations programs. Some write copy for brochures or articles before making the arrangements to have them printed, or they might use desktop publishing software to create the documents themselves. They greet clients and guide them to the proper offices, and they often supervise and train other staff members and newer secretaries, especially on how to use computer software programs.

Some secretaries perform very specialized work. *Legal secretaries* prepare legal papers including wills, mortgages, contracts, deeds, motions, complaints, and summonses. They work under the direct supervision of an attorney or paralegal. They assist with legal research by reviewing legal journals and organizing briefs for their employers. They must learn an entire specialized vocabulary that is used in legal papers and documents.

Medical secretaries take medical histories of patients, make appointments, prepare and send bills to patients (as well as track and collect them), process insurance billing, maintain medical files, and pursue correspondence with patients, hospitals, and associations. They assist physicians or medical scientists with articles, reports, speeches, and conference proceedings. Some medical secretaries are responsible for ordering medical supplies. They, too, need to learn an entire specialized vocabulary of medical terms and be familiar with laboratory or hospital procedures.

Technical secretaries work for engineers and scientists. They prepare reports and papers that often include graphics and mathematical equations that are difficult to format on paper. These secretaries maintain a technical library and help with scientific papers by gathering and editing materials.

Executive secretaries provide support for top executives. They perform fewer clerical duties and more information management-related duties, according to the *Occupational Outlook Handbook*. Their duties include managing clerical staff; assessing memos, reports, and other documents in order to determine their importance for distribution; preparing meeting agendas; and conducting research and preparing reports.

Social secretaries, often called *personal secretaries*, arrange all of the social activities of their employers. They handle private as well as business social affairs, and they may plan parties, send out invitations, or write speeches for their employers. Social secretaries often work for celebrities or high-level executives who have busy social calendars to maintain.

Many associations, clubs, and nonprofit organizations have *membership secretaries* who compile and send out newsletters or promotional materials while maintaining membership lists, dues records, and directories. Depending on the type of club, the secretary may be the one who gives out information to prospective members and who keeps current members and related organizations informed of upcoming events.

Education secretaries work in elementary or secondary schools or on college campuses. They take care of all clerical duties at the school. Their responsibilities may include preparing bulletins and reports for teachers, parents, or students, keeping track of budgets for school supplies or student activities, and maintaining the school's calendar of events. Depending on the position, they may work for school administrators, principals, or groups of teachers or professors. Other education secretaries work in administration offices, state education departments, or service departments.

REQUIREMENTS

High School
You will need at least a high school diploma to enter this field. To prepare for a career as a secretary, take high school courses including business, English, and speech. Keyboarding and computer science courses will also be helpful.

Postsecondary Training
To succeed as a secretary, you will need good office skills that include rapid and accurate keyboarding skills and good spelling and grammar. You should enjoy handling details. Some positions require typing a minimum number of words per minute, as well as shorthand ability. Knowledge of word processing, spreadsheets, and database management is important, and many employers require it. You can learn some of these skills in business education courses taught at vocational and business schools.

Certification or Licensing
Qualifying for the designation certified professional secretary rating is increasingly recognized in business and industry as a consideration for promotion as a senior level secretary. The International Association of Administrative Professionals administers the examinations required for this certification. Secretaries with limited experience can become an accredited legal secretary by obtaining certification from NALS . . . the association for legal professionals. Those with at least three years of experience in the legal field can be certified as a professional legal secretary from this same organization. Legal Secretaries International offers the certified legal secretary specialist designation in the following categories: business law, civil litigation, criminal law, intellectual property, probate, and real estate.

Other Requirements
Personal qualities are important in this field of work. As a secretary, you will often be the first employee of a company that clients meet, and therefore you must be friendly, poised, and professionally dressed. Because you must work closely with others, you should be

personable and tactful. Discretion, good judgment, organizational ability, and initiative are also important. These traits will not only get you hired but will also help you advance in your career.

Some employers encourage their secretaries to take advanced courses and to be trained to use any new piece of equipment in the office. Requirements vary widely from company to company.

EXPLORING

High school guidance counselors can give you interest and aptitude tests to help you assess your suitability for a career as a secretary. Local business schools often welcome visitors, and sometimes offer courses that can be taken in conjunction with a high school business course. Work-study programs will also provide you with an opportunity to work in a business setting to get a sense of the work performed by secretaries.

Part-time or summer jobs as receptionists, file clerks, and office clerks are often available in various offices. These jobs are the best indicators of future satisfaction in the secretarial field. You may find a part-time job if you are computer literate. Cooperative education programs arranged through schools and "temping" through an agency also are valuable ways to acquire experience. In general, any job that teaches basic office skills is helpful.

EMPLOYERS

There are 4.2 million secretaries employed throughout the United States, making this profession one of the largest in the country. Of this total, 275,000 specialize as legal secretaries and 408,000 work as medical secretaries. Secretaries are employed in almost every type of industry. Approximately 90 percent of secretaries work in service-producing industries including the legal, education, health, financial services, real estate, and business industries, as well as in retail and wholesale trade. Others work in construction and manufacturing. A large number of secretaries are employed by federal, state, and local government agencies.

STARTING OUT

Most people looking for work as secretaries find jobs through the newspaper ads or by applying directly to local businesses. Both private employment offices and state employment services place secretaries, and business schools help their graduates find suitable jobs.

Temporary-help agencies are an excellent way to find secretarial jobs, many of which may turn into permanent ones.

ADVANCEMENT

Secretaries often begin by assisting executive secretaries and work their way up by learning the way their business operates. Initial promotions from a secretarial position are usually to jobs such as secretarial supervisor, office manager, or administrative assistant. Depending on other personal qualifications, college courses in business, accounting, or marketing can help the ambitious secretary enter middle and upper management. Training in computer skills can also lead to advancement. Secretaries who become proficient in word processing, for instance, can get jobs as instructors or as sales representatives for software manufacturers.

Many legal secretaries, with additional training and schooling, become paralegals. Secretaries in the medical field can advance into the fields of radiological and surgical records or medical transcription.

EARNINGS

Salaries for secretaries vary widely by region, type of business, and the skill, experience, and level of responsibility of the secretary. Additionally, secretaries earn considerably more if certified, especially those working in the legal profession.

Secretaries (except legal, medical, and executive) earned an average annual salary of $28,220 in 2007, according to the U.S. Department of Labor. Salaries for these workers ranged from a low of $17,920 to a high of more than $42,350. Secretaries employed by the federal government earned a starting annual salary of $42,950 in 2007; those employed in local government earned $32,570.

In 2007 medical secretaries earned annual salaries that ranged from less than $20,260 to $41,860 or more, according to the U.S. Department of Labor. Legal secretaries made an average of $38,810 in 2007. Annual salaries for legal secretaries ranged from $24,380 to more than $60,800. An attorney's rank in the firm will also affect the earnings of a legal secretary; secretaries who work for a partner will earn higher salaries than those who work for an associate.

Most secretaries receive paid holidays and two weeks vacation after a year of work, as well as sick leave. Many offices provide benefits including health and life insurance, pension plans, overtime pay, and tuition reimbursement.

WORK ENVIRONMENT

Most secretaries work in pleasant offices with modern equipment. Office conditions vary widely, however. While some secretaries have their own offices and work for one or two executives, others share crowded workspace with other workers.

Most office workers work 35 to 40 hours per week. Very few secretaries work on the weekends on a regular basis, although some may be asked to work overtime if a particular project demands it.

The work is not physically strenuous or hazardous, although deadline pressure is a factor and sitting for long periods of time can be uncomfortable. Many hours spent in front of a computer can lead to eyestrain or repetitive-motion problems for secretaries. Most secretaries are not required to travel. Part-time and flexible schedules are easily adaptable to secretarial work.

OUTLOOK

The U.S. Department of Labor predicts that employment for secretaries who specialize in the medical field or who work as executive secretaries will grow faster than the average for all careers through 2016. Employment for legal secretaries and general secretaries is expected to grow about as fast as the average through 2016.

Computers, fax machines, email, copy machines, and scanners are some technological advancements that have greatly improved the work productivity of secretaries. Company downsizing and restructuring, in some cases, have redistributed traditional secretarial duties to other employees. There has been a growing trend in assigning one secretary to assist two or more managers, which has hurt the field to some extent. Although more professionals are using personal computers for their correspondence, some administrative duties will still need to be handled by secretaries. The personal aspects of the job and responsibilities such as making travel arrangements, scheduling conferences, and transmitting staff instructions have not changed.

Many employers currently complain of a shortage of capable secretaries. Those with skills and experience will have the best chances for employment. Specialized secretaries should attain certification in their field to stay competitive.

Industries such as scientific, technical, and professional services; health care and social services; and administrative and support services will create the most new job opportunities. As is common with broad occupations, the need to replace retiring workers will generate many openings.

FOR MORE INFORMATION

For information on the certified professional secretary designation, contact
International Association of Administrative Professionals
PO Box 20404
Kansas City, MO 64195-0404
Tel: 816-891-6600
Email: service@iaap-hq.org
http://www.iaap-hq.org

For information about certification, contact
Legal Secretaries International
2302 Fannin Street, Suite 500
Houston, TX 77002-9136
http://www.legalsecretaries.org

The Mayo Clinic is a major employer of medical secretaries. Visit its Web site for more information.
Mayo Clinic
http://www.mayo.edu

For information on certification, job openings, a variety of careers in law, and more, contact
NALS ... the association for legal professionals
8159 East 41st Street
Tulsa, OK 74145-3313
Tel: 918-582-5188
Email: info@nals.org
http://www.nals.org

For information regarding union representation, contact
Office and Professional Employees International Union
265 West 14th Street, Sixth Floor
New York, NY 10011-7103
Tel: 800-346-7348
http://www.opeiu.org

For employment information, contact
OfficeTeam
http://www.officeteam.com

Stock Clerks

OVERVIEW

Stock clerks receive, unpack, store, distribute, and record the inventory for materials or products used by a company, plant, or store. Approximately 1.7 million stock clerks are employed in the United States.

HISTORY

Almost every type of business establishment imaginable—shoe store, restaurant, hotel, auto repair shop, hospital, supermarket, or steel mill—buys materials or products from outside distributors and uses these materials in its operations. A large part of the company's money is tied up in these inventory stocks, but without them operations would come to a standstill. Stores would run out of merchandise to sell, mechanics would be unable to repair cars until new parts were shipped in, and factories would be unable to operate once their basic supply of raw materials ran out.

To avoid these problems, businesses have developed their own inventory-control systems to store enough goods and raw materials for uninterrupted operations, move these materials to the places they are needed, and know when it is time to order more. These systems are the responsibility of stock clerks.

QUICK FACTS

School Subjects
English
Mathematics

Personal Skills
Following instructions

Work Environment
Primarily indoors
Primarily one location

Minimum Education Level
High school diploma

Salary Range
$15,080 to $20,490 to $34,190+

Certification or Licensing
None available

Outlook
Decline

DOT
222

GOE
09.08.01

NOC
1474

O*NET-SOC
43-5081.00, 43-5081.01, 43-5081.02, 43-5081.03, 43-5081.04

THE JOB

Stock clerks work in just about every type of industry, and no matter what kind of storage or stock room they staff—food, clothing, merchandise, medicine, or raw materials—the work of stock clerks is essentially the same. They receive, sort, put away, distribute, and keep track of the items a business sells or uses. Their titles sometimes vary based on their responsibilities.

When goods are received in a stockroom, stock clerks unpack the shipment and check the contents against documents such as the invoice, purchase order, and bill of lading, which lists the contents of the shipment. The shipment is inspected, and any damaged goods are set aside. Stock clerks may reject or send back damaged items or call vendors to complain about the condition of the shipment. In large companies this work may be done by a shipping and receiving clerk.

Once the goods are received, stock clerks organize and sometimes mark them with identifying codes or prices so they can be placed in stock according to the existing inventory system. In this way the materials or goods can be found readily when needed, and inventory control is much easier. In many firms stock clerks use handheld scanners and computers to keep inventory records up to date.

In retail stores and supermarkets, stock clerks may bring merchandise to the sales floor and stock shelves and racks. In stockrooms and warehouses they store materials in bins, on the floor, or on shelves. In other settings, such as restaurants, hotels, and factories, stock clerks deliver goods when they are needed. They may do this on a regular schedule or at the request of other employees or supervisors. Although many stock clerks use mechanical equipment, such as forklifts, to move heavy items, some perform strenuous and laborious work. In general, the work of a stock clerk involves much standing, bending, walking, stretching, lifting, and carrying.

When items are removed from the inventory, stock clerks adjust records to reflect the products' use. These records are kept as current as possible, and inventories are periodically checked against these records. Every item is counted, and the totals are compared with the records on hand or the records from the sales, shipping, production, or purchasing departments. This helps identify how fast items are being used, when items must be ordered from outside suppliers, or even whether items are disappearing from the stockroom. Many retail establishments use computerized cash registers that maintain an inventory count automatically as they record the sale of each item.

The duties of stock clerks vary depending on their place of employment. Stock clerks working in small firms perform many different tasks, including shipping and receiving, inventory control, and purchasing. In large firms, responsibilities may be more narrowly defined. More specific job categories include inventory clerks, material clerks, order fillers, stock-control clerks, merchandise distributors, and shipping and receiving clerks.

A stock clerk in a warehouse moves a pallet of cookies. *(Peter Hvizdak/ The Image Works)*

At a construction site or factory that uses a variety of raw and finished materials, there are many different types of specialized work for stock clerks. *Tool crib attendants* issue, receive, and store the various hand tools, machine tools, dies, and other equipment used in an industrial establishment. They make sure the tools come back in reasonably good shape and keep track of those that need to be replaced. *Parts order and stock clerks* purchase, store, and distribute the spare parts needed for motor vehicles and other industrial equipment. *Metal control coordinators* oversee the movement of metal stock and supplies used in producing nonferrous metal sheets, bars, tubing, and alloys. In mining and other industries that regularly use explosives, *magazine keepers* store explosive materials and components safely and distribute them to authorized personnel. In the military, *space and storage clerks* keep track of the weights and amounts of ammunition and explosive components stored in the magazines of an arsenal and check their storage condition.

Many types of stock clerks can be found in other industries. *Parts clerks* handle and distribute spare and replacement parts in repair and maintenance shops. In eyeglass centers, *prescription clerks* select the lens blanks and frames for making eyeglasses and keep inventory stocked at a specified level. In motion picture companies, *property custodians* receive, store, and distribute the props needed for shooting. In hotels and hospitals, *linen room attendants* issue and keep track of inventories of bed linen, tablecloths, and uniforms, while *kitchen clerks* verify the quantity and quality of food products being taken from the storeroom to the kitchen. Aboard ships, the clerk in charge of receiving and issuing supplies and keeping track of inventory is known as the *storekeeper*.

REQUIREMENTS

High School

Although there are no specific educational requirements for beginning stock clerks, employers prefer to hire high school graduates. Reading and writing skills and a basic knowledge of mathematics are necessary; typing and filing skills are also useful. As more companies install computerized inventory systems, a knowledge of computer operations is important.

Other Requirements

Good health and good eyesight is important. A willingness to take orders from supervisors and others is necessary for this work, as is the ability to follow directions. Organizational skills also are important, as is neatness. Depending on where you work, you may be required to join a union. This is especially true of stock clerks who are employed by industry and who work in large cities with a high percentage of union-affiliated companies.

When a stock clerk handles certain types of materials, extra training or certification may be required. Generally those who handle jewelry, liquor, or drugs must be bonded.

EXPLORING

The best way to learn about the responsibilities of a stock clerk is to get a part-time or summer job as a sales clerk, stockroom helper, stockroom clerk, or, in some factories, stock chaser. These jobs are relatively easy to get and can help you learn about stock work, as well as about the duties of workers in related positions. This sort of part-time work can also lead to a full-time job.

EMPLOYERS

Approximately 1.7 million people work as stock clerks. Almost 78 percent of stock clerks work for retail and wholesale firms, and the remainder work in hospitals, factories, government agencies, schools, and other organizations. Nearly all sales floor stock clerks

are employed in retail establishments, with about two-thirds working in supermarkets.

STARTING OUT

Job openings for stock clerks often are listed in newspaper classified ads. Job seekers should contact the personnel office of the firm
looking for stock clerks and fill out an application for employment.
School counselors, parents, relatives, and friends also can be good
sources for job leads and may be able to give personal references if
an employer requires them.

Stock clerks usually receive on-the-job training. New workers
start with simple tasks, such as counting and marking stock. The
basic responsibilities of the job are usually learned within the first
few weeks. As they progress, stock clerks learn to keep records of
incoming and outgoing materials, take inventories, and place orders.
As wholesale and warehousing establishments convert to automated
inventory systems, stock clerks need to be trained to use the new
equipment. Stock clerks who bring merchandise to the sales floor
and stock shelves and sales racks need little training.

ADVANCEMENT

Stock clerks with ability and determination have a good chance of
being promoted to jobs with greater responsibility. In small firms,
stock clerks may advance to sales positions or become assistant buyers or purchasing agents. In large firms, stock clerks can advance to
more responsible stock-handling jobs, such as invoice clerk, stock
control clerk, and procurement clerk.

Furthering one's education can lead to more opportunities for
advancement. By studying at a technical or business school or taking
home-study courses, stock clerks can prove to their employer that
they have the intelligence and ambition to take on more important
tasks. More advanced positions, such as warehouse manager and
purchasing agent, are usually given to experienced people who have
post-high school education.

EARNINGS

Beginning stock clerks usually earn the minimum wage or slightly
more. The U.S. Department of Labor reports that stock clerks
earned a median annual salary of $20,490 in 2007. Experienced
stock clerks can earn anywhere from $15,080 to more than $34,190

per year, with time-and-a-half pay for overtime. Average earnings vary depending on the type of industry and geographic location. Stock clerks working in the retail trade generally earn wages in the middle range. In transportation, utilities, and wholesale businesses, earnings usually are higher; in finance, insurance, real estate, and other types of office services, earnings generally are lower.

Those working for large companies or national chains may receive excellent benefits. After one year of employment, some stock clerks are offered one to two weeks of paid vacation each year, as well as health and medical insurance and a retirement plan.

WORK ENVIRONMENT

Stock clerks usually work in relatively clean, comfortable areas. Working conditions vary considerably, however, depending on the industry and type of merchandise being handled. For example, stock clerks who handle refrigerated goods must spend some time in cold storage rooms, while those who handle construction materials, such as bricks and lumber, occasionally work outside in harsh weather. Most stock clerk jobs involve much standing, bending, walking, stretching, lifting, and carrying. Some workers may be required to operate machinery to lift and move stock.

Because stock clerks are employed in so many different types of industries, the amount of hours worked every week depends on the type of employer. Stock clerks in retail stores usually work a five-day, 40-hour week, while those in manufacturing work 44 hours, or five and one-half days, per week. Many others are able to find part-time work. Overtime is common, especially when large shipments arrive or during peak times such as holiday seasons.

OUTLOOK

Although the volume of inventory transactions is expected to increase significantly, employment for stock clerks is expected to decline through 2016, according to the U.S. Department of Labor. This is a result of increased automation and other productivity improvements that enable clerks to handle more stock. Manufacturing and wholesale trade industries are making the greatest use of automation. In addition to computerized inventory control systems, firms in these industries are expected to rely more on sophisticated conveyor belts, automatic high stackers to store and retrieve goods, and automatic guided vehicles that are battery-powered and driverless. Sales floor stock clerks probably will be less affected by automation as most of their work is done on the sales floor, where it is difficult to locate or operate complicated machinery.

Because this occupation employs a large number of workers, many job openings will occur each year to replace stock clerks who transfer to other jobs and leave the labor force. Stock clerk jobs tend to be entry-level positions, so many vacancies will be created by normal career progression.

FOR MORE INFORMATION

For information on educational programs in the retail industry, contact

National Retail Federation
325 7th Street NW, Suite 1100
Washington, DC 20004-2818
Tel: 800-673-4692
http://www.nrf.com

Index